The 'stubborn particulars' of social

psychology

KING ALFRED'S C

Stubborn Particulars' of Social Psychology gives students an alternative roach to social psychology. Because of the limits of shared under-ding often imposed by class, race, c re, nationality, ethnicity, u.ge and gender, it suggests that th an be a value-engaged way oing social psychology.

hrough a series of examples, Frances Cherry shows how categories of lysis, tools of investigation and data analysis are equally framed by orical and cultural context. She also discusses the necessity of begin-ig understand one's own biases and prejudices in a dynamic way. further illustrates how 'classic' research can be reinterpreted from a e ent perspective, and how social psychology textbooks can obscure flicts of interest and perspective.

The 'Stubborn Particulars' of Social Psychology should be required reading or all social psychology students.

Frances Cherry is Associate Professor at the Department of Psychology, Carleton University, Ottawa, Canada.

Critical Psychology
Series editors
John Broughton
Columbia University, New York
David Ingleby
University of Utrecht
Valerie Walkerdine
Goldsmiths' College, London

Since the 1960s there has been widespread disaffection with traditional approaches in psychology, and talk of a 'crisis' has been endemic. At the same time, psychology has encountered influential contemporary movements such as feminism, neo-marxism, post-structuralism and post-modernism. In this climate, various forms of 'critical psychology' have developed vigorously.

Unfortunately, such work – drawing as it does on unfamiliar intellectual traditions – is often difficult to assimilate. The aim of the Critical Psychology series is to make this exciting new body of work readily accessible to students and teachers of psychology, as well as presenting the more psychological aspects of this work to a wider social scientific audience. Specially commissioned works from leading critical writers will demonstrate the relevance of their new approaches to a wide range of current social issues.

The 'stubborn particulars' of social psychology

Essays on the research process

Frances Cherry

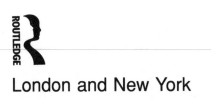

London and New York

First published 1995
by Routledge
11 New Fetter Lane, London EC4P 4EE

Simultaneously published in the USA and Canada
by Routledge
29 West 35th Street, New York, NY 10001

© 1995 Frances Cherry

Typeset in Palatino by
Florencetype Ltd, Stoodleigh, Devon

Printed and bound in Great Britain by
Biddles Ltd, Guildford and King's Lynn

British Library Cataloguing in Publication Data
A catalogue record for this book is available from the British Library

Library of Congress Cataloging in Publication Data
A catalog record for this book has been requested

ISBN 0–415–06666–2 (hbk)
ISBN 0–415–06667–0 (pbk)

Contents

For Douglas Yuill, applied synergist

Acknowledgements

This book reflects a transformation in my understanding of social psychology over a twenty-year period. Over these years, my commitment to an historical understanding of how we have constructed research subjects, practices and topics in social psychology has resulted in my involvement with a delightful group of maverick souls. You will find us in various overlapping configurations at the annual meetings of Section 25, History and Philosophy of Psychology of the Canadian Psychological Association; at the annual meetings of Division 26, History of Psychology of the American Psychological Association; at the biannual meetings of the International Society for Theoretical Psychology; at Cheiron and Cheiron Europe meetings; and at the American-based Forum for the History of Human Sciences in the History of Science Society. I am grateful to so many of these itinerant scholars who make their way to annual meetings to push forward critical and reconstructive efforts in psychology: Erika Apfelbaum, Betty Bayer, Kurt Danziger, Laurel Furumoto, Ken and Mary Gergen, Barry Kelly, Ian Lubek, Henry Minton, Jill Morawski, Mary Parlee, Tim Rogers, Franz Samelson, Hank Stam and Charles Tolman.

Along the way I have been fortunate to meet people who have helped me grow intellectually, emotionally and spiritually. I am indebted to David Bakan, Ron Ballentine, Donn Byrne, Marcia Chambers, Christina Cole, Judith Davis, Kay Deaux, Susan Glass, John Gottman, Fran Klodawsky, Sally and Bob Luce, Marva Major, Marilyn Marshall, Ann Mully, Kristen Ostling, Rob Richardson, Maria Rukiewicz, Lloyd Strickland, Warren Thorngate and Jo Wood. I am grateful beyond measure to my teacher and friend, Frances Itani, for her classes and her profound understanding of the science of fiction and the art of non-fiction.

I have been privileged over the years to work with extraordinary students and several of their insights are represented in the pages of this book. Special thanks are extended to Debby Anderson, Cathy Borshuk, Judith Kalin, Mark Lajoie, Ian Nicholson, Tim Pychyl and Steve Zikopoulos, who have been a constant incentive to bring this book to completion.

I will probably never recover from the mother-guilt of abandoning some idealized version of domestic life with my son, Daniel, in favour of the isolation and eccentric habits required to write. But his well-timed acts of indifference, complaint, humour and appreciation have at least kept me centred and able to laugh at myself. Words of thanks go to Else Brock and Penny Lange, whose assistance with the manuscript preparation preserved my mental health and to Valerie Walkerdine, whose clear-headed persistence has worked to bring this project to completion. Thanks to John Broughton and Routledge staff – Emma Cotter and Bradley Scott – for their instructive editorial work.

And a final thank you to my first family for giving me the gift of seeing things from different points of view.

I would like to acknowledge the following for permission to use previously published and unpublished materials: The Literary Trust of Bronwen Wallace for use of the phrase 'stubborn particulars' from Bronwen Wallace (1987) *The Stubborn Particulars of Grace*, Toronto: McClelland and Stewart; Harvard University Archives for use of unpublished material from the Gordon Allport papers presented in Chapter 1; Rick Goodwin, John Macdonald and Sherry Galey for use of the text of the poster presented in Chapter 3, p. 36; *Science* magazine for permission to reprint Figure 1 (reproduced in this volume as Figure 4.1, p. 42) from D.A. Jenni and M.A. Jenni (1976) 'Carrying behavior in humans: analysis of sex differences', © 1976 by the AAAS; D.B. Lynn and A. De Palma Cross for providing the raw data from their 1974 study 'Parent preference of preschool children', published in *Journal of Marriage and the Family*, p. 558, and adapted for use in this volume in Tables 4.1 and 4.2, Chapter 4, p. 49; Stanford University Press for use of figures, photograph and extensive quotations in Chapter 6 from L. Festinger, S. Schachter and K. Back (1950) *Social Pressures in Informal Groups*; HarperCollins Publishers, Inc. for permission to reprint Table 11.1 (reproduced in this volume as Table 8.1, p. 104, from Muzafer Sherif and Carolyn W. Sherif, *Social Psychology*, New York: 3rd Edition, © 1969 by Muzafer and Carolyn W. Sherif.

Joss Mackennan could not be located. It is my understanding that he was the designer for the poster reprinted in Chapter 3, p. 32.

Introduction

This set of eight essays is about the historical and cultural specificity of social psychological research. I have used each essay to demonstrate that the practice of social psychology requires a continuous reconciliation of the particulars of social life with the more general and multiple frameworks we might bring to bear on our understanding of these particulars. In each essay, I have experimented with the balance between the researcher's interpretive framework and those social events that are taken to be central to the meaningfulness of that framework.

Unlike much of contemporary social psychology, I have chosen paradox, incompleteness and uncertainty as my working assumptions. I take social psychology to be an interpretive science that depends in significant ways on the life experiences of the social psychologist. These essays are mindful of the limits of shared understanding often imposed by class, race, culture, nationality, ethnicity, language and gender. In many of these essays, I have enlarged the number of perspectives on a problem, an experiment, or a phenomenon in order to loosen the intellectual grip of looking at things in one way. All of these essays are prolegomena for enhancing the more general habit of multiple perspective-taking that I believe must form the basis of social justice and social change.

Through the writing of this book I have come to think of myself as a 'post-crisis' social psychologist where crisis has meant a turning point that sent me off in directions other than my formal training as an experimental social psychologist. These directions have included the history of social psychology, sociology of knowledge, feminist critiques of science and the interface of social science and literature. Each of these directions has raised questions about the kind of knowledge psychological social psychology provides and in whose different interests this research is conducted.

Each chapter of this book is stylistically an essay that examines an aspect of the production of social psychological knowledge. To write in this way I had to think and write past the kinds of formats, such as a journal article or technical report, that my training had prepared me to follow. For several years, I experimented with various kinds of writing and narrative forms of expression. At times, I felt very annoyed with myself that I could not fit the mould of my original training. At other times, I felt angry with the routine way in which social psychology was practised. Hindsight suggests that the conflict provided the creative tension I needed to make sense of social psychology in my own way.

This group of essays begins with the history of social psychology itself and an analysis of the overwhelming commitment the field has to presenting itself as an experimental science (Chapter 1). I have looked for some exceptions to the rule that raise other ways of practising social psychology. Since students are introduced in their first year of studying psychology to a sequenced approach to the research process, namely, hypothesis generation, data collection, analysis and write-up of results, I have organized the essays to reflect aspects of this sequence.

Chapters 2 and 3 are intended to examine the specificity of theorizing and hypothesis generation. Here the focus is on the interconnection between science and politics in the formulation of social research. I have made use of research on violence towards women as I cannot think of an area in which the paradigms of social psychology are as often in conflict with alternative knowledge constructions. There are two particular case studies I have used. The first involves the 1964 murder of Kitty Genovese in Queens, New York while the second involves the 1989 murders of fourteen women at an engineering school in Montreal.

My intention in Chapter 4 was to show by several concrete examples in the area of sex-role identity how categories of analysis, tools of investigation and data analysis are equally framed by historical and cultural context. Our research practices are never exercised in value-free ways and part of our task as researchers is to begin to specify the values that frame our research questions, methods and interpretations. In Chapter 5, I have tried to chart my own perspective shifts and the way they continue to influence my practice of social psychology. It would be naive to think that I understand myself so thoroughly that each and every bias and prejudice I hold has been explored in this book. What is more hopeful is that I have modelled a dynamic practice of reflexivity and dialogue that might be useful to students when they approach seemingly static social texts.

In Chapter 6, I have used one of social psychology's 'classics', Festinger's Westgate housing studies, to show just how challenging but potentially liberating it can be to reinterpret research from a different perspective. I have tried to stress the unfinished business of research and knowledge production. Consequently, when it comes to publishing and communicating social psychology to students, textbooks and research articles need to be read critically as versions of social problem-solving rather than as received truths (Chapter 7). I have not concluded from the possibility of multiple interpretations of the social world that we should give up hope of ever understanding anything. Rather, multiple interpretations are necessary to understanding that social science research has been as much about social control and power as about human emancipation.

In many ways, these essays are a retrospective account of the way I've come to expect something extra from social psychology – that it be a self-reflexive and value-explicit social science. I continue to build a social psychology that is politically engaged by working with minority perspectives. To that end, my work of researching, writing, analysing and teaching seeks to transform the curriculum by including those people (and perspectives) previously denied access to knowledge production as students, researchers, writers and teachers. Stretching well beyond this book, my larger goal is to raise the standards of inclusivity in the Academy.

Most of what is social psychology is what teachers of social psychology practise in their classrooms and research programmes whenever they address a social issue. In our practice we are continually modelling for others and to ourselves ways of making sense. Kidder and Fine (1986) have challenged social scientists to move away from making sense of injustice in the 'individual deficits and missed opportunities' that members of any particular marginalized group have experienced and, instead, to make sense of injustice as part of 'societal conflicts of interest'. That shift of perspective challenges the consciousness of academic social psychologists to 'deprivatize' and 'deindividualize' social injustice and to see that they have a role to play in transforming consciousness and, ultimately, social action. Kidder and Fine write:

> Social research can demonstrate contradictions in social experience, discrepancies between public ideologies and social practices, and the gaps in experience reported by those in high- and low-power positions. Social scientists can document and legitimate the voices of those most intimately affected by social injustice . . . . Neither social scientists nor practitioners can continue to collude in obscuring the context, riddled with conflicts of interests, from which social injustices derive.
> (Kidder and Fine 1986: 60–1)

In Chapter 8, I make use of another of social psychology's classic studies, in this case the work of Muzafer Sherif and his colleagues, to show how the teaching of social psychology across several decades through textbooks can indeed come to obscure conflicts of interest and perspective. I have included in the text suggested exercises that might be useful to those who teach social psychology and would like to involve students with the approach I have taken. It is my hope that these essays generate another way of practising social psychology.

Chapter 1

Are you a 'real' scientist?

> While the modern social psychologist does indeed need experimental, statistical, and computer skills, he needs also historical perspective. He needs immersion in theories (both macro and micro). Above all, he needs an ability to relate his problem to the context in which it properly belongs. Sometimes the context lies in the traditions of academic psychology, often in sociology or anthropology, sometimes in philosophy or theology, occasionally in history or in economics, frequently in the political life of our day. Sometimes the science of genetics or clinical experience provides the context.
>
> (Allport 1966: 17)[1]

Soon after I received my Doctor of Philosophy degree in 1974, I had what I thought was a peculiar encounter. A man sitting next to me in an airport lounge must have noticed the 'Dr' in front of my name on my luggage tag. He caught my attention and asked me what kind of doctor I was. What I remember was that he took his wrist pulse in a very automatic way while he asked me. I answered with equal ease 'Not the kind that takes the pulse'. We smiled and lapsed back into silence. It was almost as if that small gesture were *the* behavioural indicator differentiating the 'real' doctor from an imposter. Real doctors take the pulse, prescribe drugs, and treat the physical body and presumably it was medical advice that my fellow traveller was seeking. To him I was that other kind of 'doctor'. I might have been a clinical psychologist generally identified with treating the minds of troubled persons and sometimes suspected of knowing what a person is really thinking. When conversations such as these continue and I put forth that I am a social psychologist, I am frequently confronted with a sort of 'Oh, that's nice dear' kind of smile. If I explore the other person's everyday hunch about what it is I do, various intriguing guesses arise – a 'doctor' of the social pulse, a pollster and, once, a census taker.

Well, if those I meet on my travels aren't very sure what a social psychologist is or does, one would expect that at least within the world of the Academy it is somewhat clearer. Yet even here, questions of self-definition often troubled and preoccupied social psychologists to the extent that a literature of 'crisis' developed throughout the 1970s (Elms

1975; Gergen 1973; Israel and Tajfel 1972; Strickland *et al*. 1976). At the core of these writings were concerns about how best to conceptualize the work of social psychologists. Are we to see ourselves primarily as scientists, practitioners, teachers, social activists or social critics?

I was preoccupied during my graduate school years and for at least a decade after with these matters of definition, not surprisingly because they are bound up with theories about what counts as knowledge, how research should be done, and what techniques for gathering evidence are allowable (Harding 1987). This series of essays is about a transition in my way of understanding social psychology. Each essay reflects another way in which I have come to practise a social psychology that is grounded in historical and cultural contexts. For me, the study of experimental social psychology that I began in 1970 has connected to a larger story of the history of psychology and the social sciences.

One part of the history of social psychology involves the emergence of a particular model of human activity that gathers momentum in the Enlightenment period of European intellectual development (Venn 1984). Mind itself became a natural object detached from social relations. As mind became an object with measurable properties the stage was set for the practice of a social psychology about persons as interacting objects, similar to the interaction of objects in nature. A view of minds (and persons) capable of being studied out of their historical and social context fostered a set of research practices that focused increasingly on quantifiable accounts of individual action. The approach has been variously understood as mechanistic and ahistorical, influenced deeply by the models within general experimental psychology, which itself was modelled on a nineteenth-century understanding of the physical world (Brandt 1982).

The history of how and why North American psychological science arrived at models of representing human activity taken from the natural and physical sciences is beyond the scope of this book. Indeed, the mystification of social psychology as a 'real' experimental science and its location in systems of social engineering and control are the subject of much recent research in the philosophy of social science, feminist psychology, history and the sociology of psychological knowledge (Apfelbaum 1986; Collier *et al*. 1991; Danziger 1990; Henriques *et al*. 1984; Lubek 1993a; Morawski 1988; Parker 1989; Wilkinson, S. 1986).

My simpler purpose in this essay is to look at the stories that are currently told to incoming undergraduate students about what social psychology is and how it came to be. The stories are best told in introductory textbook accounts of social psychology's past and through 'histories' of the discipline more often read by graduate students. These are powerful devices for constructing our collective identity as scientists rather than philosophers, researchers rather than political activists.

THE DISCOVERY OF HISTORY[2]

Until quite recently, Gordon Allport's history of social psychology was the main source for anyone interested in the origins and definition of the field. His 'Historical background of modern social psychology' first appeared in the 1954 *Handbook of Social Psychology* (Allport 1954). It was reprinted in the 1968 *Handbook* with minor modifications throughout the text and a new conclusion (Allport 1968a). In the 1985 *Handbook*, it was retained with some modifications (Allport 1985). Originally, Allport wrote a history of ideas or concepts that had emerged in post-Second World War social psychology. His historical presentation celebrated continuity and progress as social psychology developed from philosophical speculation to scientific respectability. For example, a concept used in the present, such as 'reinforcement theory', is seen as a more scientific restatement of an earlier philosophical notion, in this case Jeremy Bentham's 'hedonism' (Allport 1954: 10–13). Allport maintained that '(O)ur intellectual ancestors, for all their fumbling, were asking precisely the same questions that we are asking today' (Allport 1954: 3). He wrote that '(W)ith few exceptions, social psychologists regard their discipline as *an attempt to understand and explain how the thought, feeling, and behavior of individuals are influenced by the actual, imagined, or implied presence of others'* (emphasis in original, Allport 1954: 5).

Allport's historical vantage point has been criticized for its presentation of a false continuity with earlier thinkers such as Auguste Comte (Samelson 1974). It can be argued also that it constructs a narrative with an overly presentist and ethnocentric bias. Allport wrote that 'A study of the history of social psychology can be justified only if it shows the relevance of historical backgrounds to present-day foregrounds' (Allport 1954: 1), and that social psychology reached its peak in America because 'It seems that in the United States, the soil of western thought, fortified by practical meliorism, proved most fertile for the assertive growth of social psychology and related disciplines' (Allport 1954: 4). Allport celebrated American social psychology's objectivity while he saw the emerging Russian social psychology as ideologically biased (Allport 1954: 47–8). Allport's history served to legitimate social psychology as a pragmatic, coherent and progressive experimental science aimed at the prediction and control of social behaviour. Yet, Allport came to have concerns about extreme positivism. By the second edition, he lamented that 'The arrival of the positivism that Comte advocated has led to an essentially non-theoretical orientation' (Allport 1968a: 69) and that the over-production of 'snippets of empiricism' (Allport 1968a: 68) was not a good sign. As mentioned above, his history was included in the third edition of the *Handbook of Social Psychology* (Allport 1985) but the critiques brought to bear by theoretical and historical scholarship were not referenced or acknowledged. The section on Auguste Comte was simply excised.

Archival work in the Allport Papers at Harvard University Archives provided me with a better sense of how Allport's history of social psychology evolved. As Gardner Lindzey and Eliot Aronson set to work (in 1963) on the second edition of the *Handbook*, Allport was given the opportunity to revise his history and was asked to write a chapter on current trends in the field. He was satisfied for the most part with his historical analysis and had his manuscript to the editors by May 1965. It was copy-edited by a student in 1967 as Allport was by then too ill to do this task. He died on 9 October 1967. While he had declined the task of writing a 'current trends' chapter for the 1968 *Handbook*, he did present a paper entitled 'Six decades of social psychology' at a Conference on the Teaching of Social Psychology in December 1966. The conference was held in New York under the auspices of the National Science Foundation and the Division of Personality and Social Psychology of the American Psychological Association. Allport's paper was subsequently published in the conference's edited proceedings (Allport 1968b).

In Allport's conference presentation, he expressed serious concerns about a social psychology that developed without attention to history or context. His 1968 *Handbook* chapter is worthy of understanding in contrast to this conference paper;[3] the former has much to do with Allport's love of grand recurring themes in the history of thought and what he called in his conference paper 'an appropriate eclecticism in psychological theory' (Allport 1966: 5). In the conference paper, Allport expressed his concerns more strongly that the student was being 'fed fragments, not theory' (Allport 1966: 13) and that the 1950s and 1960s predisposed us to 'inflate our methods into "methodologies" because we are so conscious of them and so childishly proud' (Allport 1966: 11). He spoke of this obsession with methods that 'seems to betoken a drift whose significance is not yet fully clear' (Allport 1966: 11). While still attached to 'clear methods', 'an accurate handling of data', 'severe self-scrutiny in research' (Allport 1966: 11) and as an optimist to the end about what science could offer society, Allport none the less concluded that 'We do well to face frankly our failure thus far to demonstrate our claim to be a powerful theoretical and applied social science' (Allport 1966: 15).

In Allport's view, social psychology was a young science and had become sidetracked by endless empiricism. He reported his observation that 94 per cent of the references in articles in the July and August issues of the *Journal of Personality and Social Psychology* for 1966 were to work done after 1950. His caution to students anticipated the oncoming crisis, even if he was too ambivalent and diplomatic to take a stand in print. The following passage in the unpublished version (Allport 1966) was omitted from the published version (Allport 1968b) as 'too censorious':

And so my final word is this: Let no student think that by grinding out a hasty dissertation to refute some equally hasty dissertation of the previous year, he becomes thereby a permanently trained and qualified social psychologist – not even if his dissertation scintillates with an awesome 'methodology'.

(Allport 1966: 17)

What followed in the second chapter of the *Handbook*'s third edition was a lengthy piece by E.E. Jones (1985a) entitled 'Major developments in social psychology during the past five decades'. Unlike Allport, his goal was to survey a shorter past. He planned to 'concentrate on American social psychology with only occasional references to European developments' (Jones, E.E. 1985a: 47) in a time-frame involving post-Second World War social psychology as practised within the disciplinary infrastructure of psychology. While he acknowledged that 'many outstanding contributors to the field were European refugees' (Jones, E.E. 1985a: 47), without a deeper historical treatment Jones, among others, could not explain '(W)hy Lewin was invited to the Iowa Child Welfare Station in 1934 or why attribution theory flowered in Kansas, to which Fritz Heider moved in 1947' (Jones, E.E. 1985a: 54).[4]

By excising social psychology's temporal and spatial history, the field was inevitably distorted. Other cultures were made to appear static and backward:

> Social psychology would be less prominent, if it existed at all, in more homogeneous and traditional cultures. In such cultures behavior priorities within settings are rather well established by unquestioned cultural norms. Conflict is minimal as everyone more or less follows the traditional ways. The presence of competing normative options may account, in part, for the distinctive flowering of social psychology in the United States.

(Jones, E.E. 1985a: 53)

Within the American context, his focus on social psychology as a product of large urban universities forced distortions on the rest of American society. It was in the cities, he argued, that 'problems of intergroup conflict, prejudice, deviance, and attitudinal differences were the most salient. Indeed, a rural social psychology is almost a contradiction in terms' (Jones, E.E. 1985a: 53).

Social psychology was contextualized historically by Jones as inherently liberal and progressive, a 'troublesome disrupter of the status quo' (Jones, E.E. 1985a: 53) but those parts of its history that have either been more radical or more preserving of the *status quo* were missing. Why this narrowing of focus in all aspects of social psychology's history?

My reading of this 'history' is that it was written to serve a particular purpose, namely, to legitimate the social psychologist as a 'real' scientist. Within the context of the discipline of psychology, Jones applauded the arrival in the late 1960s of social psychology as modestly respectable given 'additional impetus stemming from a new perception of social psychology as constructively linked to the experimental method and therefore entitled to a place in the psychological mainstream' (Jones, E.E. 1985a: 54). It remains to be seen whether Jones's reconstructions of the antecedents of many fields of social psychological inquiry will withstand the test of historical scholarship. What is clear is that the real social psychologist is a scientist.

In an overlapping paper (Jones, E.E. 1985b) entitled 'History of social psychology', the discipline as an expression of a natural science model was more succinctly framed. In that paper, Jones took issue with Allport's 'impressive continuity in the problem focus of nineteenth-century social theorists and contemporary investigators' (Jones, E.E. 1985b: 373). The central advance brought by the 'availability of experimentation as a research paradigm' (Jones, E.E. 1985b: 374) was the cornerstone of what Jones took to have been progress in the field. The false start with Wilhelm Wundt's disbelief that there could be an experimental social psychology was overturned. Jones wrote: 'sometimes people don't get the word, labels are ignored, and new paths are opened as if by accident' (Jones, E.E. 1985b: 374). Triplett's experiment in 1898; Floyd Allport's behav- iouristic textbook *Social Psychology* published in 1924, followed by other milestones in social measurement; experimental method; and even the rise of theory were selected to represent advancement (Jones, E.E. 1985b: 375–7 and *passim*).

All of this led Jones to conclude that the challenge to social psychology in the 1970s posed by a literature that suggested a crisis in social psychology of intellectual, ethical and practical significance was not fundamental. The acceptance of a naturalistic metaphysic remained unshaken although he acknowledged that 'There is an articulate minority of social psychologists who may view my remarks as the dying gasp of a maladaptive breed and who question the very possibility of effective and illuminating experimentation on social psychological processes' (Jones, E.E. 1985b: 404). Jones remained convinced that one could best under- stand social life with the present 'cumulative, objective, science of social behavior' that has the 'special advantages of control, quantification and comparison' (Jones, E.E. 1985b: 404). Jones's 'history' tells a story of discontinuity. It is less a history and more a polemic; it is a story about how social psychology became a 'real' science, how much better off we are than in the pre-scientific days gone by and why it is important to stay the way we are.

Telling the history of social psychology as a story about continuous progress from the pre-scientific past or as a story about an enlightened present that is discontinuous with the past allows for two self-conceits. In the first case, one can take pride in having the good sense to join in the march of progress, that is to be on the winning team. In the second case, one can revel in how much more modern one is than the superstitious ancestors. Both versions bolster the view of the social psychologist as arrived, that is, as a 'real' scientist.

Not everyone has abandoned the possibility of an historically contextualized social psychology. For example, Carl Graumann in his 'Introduction to a history of social psychology' starts out with the question 'Why study history?'. Concerning disciplinary history, he argues that:

> We *can* learn from history, if it has not exclusively been written for identificatory and justificatory purposes as is mainly the case in 'presentist' history. In order to be useful a history of a discipline must allow for the discontinuities, drawbacks, failures and dead ends as well as for continuity, success and progress. It must not pretend unity if there is pluralism as in social psychology. . . . For disciplinary history the context is not only the system of sciences, but the social, political, and economic system within which an individual discipline develops.
>
> (Graumann 1988: 4–5, emphasis in original)

Graumann locates social psychology in the broader context of social philosophy and argues that 'The decision how far to extend the past or the history of social psychology and whom to include is a function of a writer's present conception of the social and the psychological' (Graumann 1988: 5). His acknowledgement of pluralism begins to tell us that there are several histories. Graumann would likely agree that the answers to why Lewin was in Iowa, Heider in Kansas, or Tajfel in England, require an historical examination of Hitler's Europe that 'emptied most of Europe of whoever and whatever there was in social psychology' (Graumann 1988: 15). Indeed, Graumann achieves a reconstruction of a pluralistic social psychology by contrasting its development in America with European social psychology before and after the Second World War. Social psychology developed within the context of world political and economic events: the Depression years in the United States; Hitler's murder of European intellectuals or their forced migration; and the American economic reconstruction of Europe after the war. By examining the long past of social inquiry and the stubborn particulars of how social psychology has been practised in different cultural and institutional contexts, one can then say more of what the 'history' of social psychology has been.

What is called for is critical historical work about disciplinary development that would include an analysis of traditional historical authorities, of the historians' own assumptions and of the assumption that the discipline has followed a steady path to progress (Danziger 1984). Critical historical work can show us, for example, that the very debate about the role of the social psychologist as political activist or detached scientist has a long history and preoccupied discussion in the 1920s and 1930s in a manner similar to the 1970s (Minton 1984; Nicholson 1991). Similarly, an even stronger critical historiography pushes us to look at the very objects of our study, as phenomena that 'do not occur in nature as raw givens but are the product of human construction' (Danziger 1984: 100). This allows for the possibility of examining the psychological objects of social psychology in the context of the social interests that are served by them.

Current pedagogical practices for introducing social psychology to large numbers of students frequently sidestep the historical dimension. Textbooks are now the primary resource for pedagogy in social psychology, especially in North America. They tell the contemporary story of social psychology as an experimental science and of the social psychologist as an experimental scientist (Lubek 1993b). Despite evidence to the contrary, textbooks provide the 'origin myths' for discussing Comte as the founding father of social psychology, McDougall's social psychology text as the first one in the field, and Triplett's experiment as the first in experimental social psychology (Haines and Vaughan 1979; Rudmin 1985; Samelson 1974). The presentation of social psychology as a cumulative science, originating from founding fathers, texts or classic studies and continuously making progress and new discoveries is conveyed in such a routine way that textbooks become a standardized and uncritical form of pedagogy.

Textbooks in social psychology have been acknowledged as the most pervasive means of communicating the discipline to incoming students. Alcock wrote that our textbooks served two main purposes, 'first to transmit knowledge from one generation to the next, and second, to inculcate specific values in its students, even though these values are often taught without conscious awareness by the teacher' (Alcock 1978: 2). Jones, in his review of five decades of social psychological research, noted that 'textbooks in social psychology have played a distinctive role in shaping and integrating the field' (Jones, E.E. 1985a: 49). He further wrote that 'It is hard to think of another field in which textbooks have served as such an important vehicle for theorizing about, and generating influential distinctions within their subject matter' (Jones, E.E. 1985a: 49). Textbooks themselves provide us with a rich archival source of our philosophical and cultural values as well as evidence of our preferred research practices. They are part of building a socio-historical understanding of social psychology.

To gain a better understanding of the metatheoretical positions expressed in textbooks of social psychology, Ellen Corkery[5] and I undertook a study of thirty textbooks published between 1925 and 1985 selected from the list provided in Jones's review paper (Jones, E.E. 1985a). For her part of the analysis, she used a content analysis that differentiated a naturalistic from an historical conception of science (Levine 1976). Corkery examined the textbooks to see which, if either, of these approaches was predominant in textbooks of social psychology. Levine had previously used this distinction to examine research in journals of social psychology that were psychologically or sociologically based. He noted that the two conceptions of science both assumed that there is an orderly social world that can be known through systematic study. Beyond that, the naturalistic and the historical conceptions were differentiated by assumptions made respectively about stability rather than variability of social behaviour, the researcher's values as separate from rather than part of the research process, and the ahistorical and lawful nature of social behaviour rather than its context and time-dependent nature. These contrasting themes were intensified in the 'crisis' literature that developed in the mid-1970s but Corkery and I had a hunch that the contrast would not be reflected explicitly in the messages conveyed to incoming students of the discipline. In actuality, mention of social psychology's history in our survey of textbooks was scant, largely drawing on Allport's (1968a) history of the discipline, and stressing the empiricist philosophers, the early textbooks by McDougall and Ross in 1908, or the earliest experiment by Triplett. Current knowledge was presented as cumulative and progressive, and fewer authors (e.g. Sampson 1971) explicitly noted the discontinuous and historically contingent nature of the discipline. A 'crisis' or period of re-examination in social psychology was mentioned in three of the six texts that covered the period from 1970 on (Secord and Backman 1964; Shaver 1977; Wrightsman and Deaux 1981).

In fact, Corkery found that while all of the textbooks were attempts at systematic inquiry into the order of social behaviour, a full two-thirds of them adopted the naturalistic conception of science for pursuing this inquiry. At the outset (often in an introductory chapter), the textbook authors took special care to qualify social psychology as 'scientific', 'experimental', and 'objective', and to include in subsequent chapters primarily experimental laboratory research to support this view. About 50 per cent of the textbook authors presented social psychology as a natural rather than an historical science by augmenting their introductory comments with a characterization of the basic principles of science *per se*, using descriptors such as 'objective', 'value-free', 'reliable', 'experimental' and 'ahistorical' and using descriptions of the goals and ideals of scientific practice. Other techniques used to legitimate social psychology as a natural science rather than an historical one involved an emphasis on quantification and a distinction made between social psychology and other fields of social inquiry: sociology, anthropology, philosophy or history itself.

In textbooks where authors used terms such as 'culturally dependent' and 'value-laden', they often went on to argue for cross-cultural

investigations to ensure the universality of social principles or to advo-
cate methodological innovations to reduce or eliminate biases from
research. The idea was not acknowledged that hypothesis generation and
data gathering were themselves social activities bound by one's cultural
context. Neither was the idea that biases in our investigative practices are
something we cannot get rid of and thereby achieve an objective
measuring standard.[6]

Our investigative practices grow out of particular cultural and social
circumstances and, while cultural values can be made explicit, they
remain an integral part of the research process. Thus, 'Investigative practices do much more than order observations of a world that is given – they
actually prepare the world that is there to be observed' (Danziger 1990:
195). Experimental investigation with human subjects, constructed in textbooks as the mark of 'real' science because it affords the experimenter
'control', has itself a long and varied history and is itself subject to sociocultural meanings. Danziger writes:

> [H]uman subjects in psychological experiments are in fact unable to
> behave simply as natural objects. Even if they try to do so, which
> depends entirely on their appraisal of the social situation they are in,
> they negate this fictional goal in the very act of trying to reach it,
> because such efforts represent an exercise of their social agency.
> Psychological experiments are therefore different in principle from
> experiments in physics because the experimenter and the human data
> source must necessarily be engaged in a social relationship. This is no
> 'artifact' but one of the essential preconditions of having a viable
> experimental situation.
>
> (Danziger 1990: 9)

In departments of psychology, the practice of social psychology legitimated itself professionally through the techniques already established in
the medical and physical sciences of the nineteenth century. It was the
human subject as natural object rather than as active participant that
emerged and took root in North American laboratories in the early part
of the twentieth century. While there was considerable variation in investigative practices, the relationship between the person and society with
which we currently work became highly stylized in the experimental
social psychology practised during the 1950s to 1970s. This period
reflected the natural science conception of social psychology that saw the
use of investigative practices as value-neutral tools. More consistent with
the historical conception was the notion that investigative practices were
themselves social and historical products.

Despite the consistency of Corkery's sample of textbooks in conveying
a naturalistic rather than an historical conception of science, there were
important exceptions that I discovered by reading the textbooks' prefaces,

a section that revealed the variety of reasons textbook authors gave for writing their books. Prefaces[7] formed a narrative account of how a social psychologist wanted to present the world in the pages that followed. Quite frequently the author would write in the third person, 'the author(s)', which had the effect of creating greater distance, impersonality and the detached objectivity more appropriate to the assumptions of the naturalistic conception of social science. Other prefaces revealed exceptions.

From reading prefaces I learned that the range of stated goals in textbooks before the mid-1970s was quite broad. Authors of social psychology textbooks wrote to present a specific orientation such as field theory, symbolic interactionism or social psychology as an extension of the principles of general psychology. They wrote to convey what they took to be the unique subject material of social psychology, be that person perception or group dynamics. Some authors wrote their textbooks to improve upon existing material or to 'upgrade' the material. Secord and Backman wrote:

> We believe that the first course in social psychology should be upgraded. We have experimented with 'toughening' introductory social psychology ... and the results, even for students of average ability, are encouraging ... In our opinion, a course which presents 'watered-down' material, which emphasizes practical affairs at the expense of scientific knowledge and methodology, and which omits the more difficult literature does a disservice to the student and to the field of social psychology. Upgrading the subject as this book does should produce a course which is no more difficult than many others taught in the junior year, such as advanced courses in the natural sciences.
>
> (Secord and Backman 1964: Preface)

In contrast, another author surveyed students' preferences for materials of interest, the personal importance of the topic and its help in understanding their own social relationships, and the intellectually stimulating nature of the material. One might expect this to be a textbook of the 1960s but in fact, it was Bird's social psychology textbook of 1940 (Bird 1940).

Whereas textbooks throughout the 1980s became more standardized and focused on comprehensive reviews of research, earlier models were more personal and selective, attempting to make the social psychologist's task more intelligible in some systematic way. Among the textbooks of the 1970s were a few written in the first person and reflecting something closer to an historical conception of social science (Elms 1972; Sampson 1971; Samuel 1975). Some of these textbooks were challenges to the prevailing and quickly solidifying dominance of the natural science conception of social psychology. Sampson warned that 'a text often makes more sense out of a field than there really is' (Sampson 1971:

Preface) and stated that his goal was to interest students in a field in which their reading might lead to action. In subsequent chapters on the American student and black protest movements of the 1960s he dispelled the notion of value-free knowledge by including an account of his own involvement and sympathies for these social movements. He wrote, 'I do not trust anyone who purports to discuss these controversial topics but disclaims bias or personal interest' (Sampson 1971: 357). He argued for considering the observer's framework if one wants to understand the judgements being made in any area of social research and that this is no less true for the textbook author than the subject of research on social perception and judgement. Some of the biases in any textbook account are 'conscious knowns' while others are 'a hodgepodge of more or less unconscious motives, dreams, and blinding defenses' (Sampson 1971: 357).

Likewise, Elms began his textbook with an 'immodest chapter' in which he expressed his personal and professional commitments in social psychology:

> During my undergraduate years, I knew few students besides myself who looked for relevance in their courses. When I found it, I took it as a bonus, over and above the pleasures of the scholarly games to which my professors seemed devoted. But even as I continued to search, a large new audience of undergraduates were growing up to demand relevance as their due. Students' demands have become an occupational hazard of college teaching, but this is one I can welcome.
>
> (Elms 1972: 2)

Futhermore, Elms intended to write about areas of research with which he had first-hand personal involvement and in 'nontechnical terms, in hopes that they may gain a wider audience among concerned laymen, whether in or out of college' (Elms 1972: 2). In this way he let the reader know that he was writing 'a distinctly personal book, rather than an impartial survey of social psychology' and that 'It won't always be possible to make sense of the data' (Elms 1972: 10).

C.W. Sherif's textbook, *Orientation in Social Psychology* (1976) was an even stronger example of a textbook reflecting an historical approach. Sherif began with the premise that social psychological knowledge reflected not a set of accumulated facts but a way of going about knowing. She emphasized research as a process not an outcome. Social behaviour was not neatly and tidily understood through unchanging laws but rather it was the way in which some individuals found it useful to approach persistently pressing problems in society. It was one way of making the world intelligible that was itself embedded in an historical and cultural context. The newcomer to social psychology was not provided with a discrete set of facts and findings in Sherif's textbook but rather with an approach filtered through a personal vision, without being simply anecdotal or unsystematic.

C.W. Sherif prefaced her book by reflecting on her purpose in writing it. She wrote, 'I started writing this book because I wanted to help newcomers find their bearings in social psychology' (Sherif 1976: xi). She went on to say, 'In all conscience, I could not write about social psychology as an established, coherent body of "knowledge" that I could parcel out in neat bundles' (Sherif 1976: xi). She would not include a complete summary of research but rather her aim would be to show how research comes into being. In this regard, she did not present a view of herself as the objective social scientist putting knowledge into the heads of eager students. She presented herself more as a model for how anyone might go about trying to make sense of complex issues of social behaviour.

Sherif stressed that all knowledge is filtered through a conscious self in interaction with others and that science is best understood as a personal process. This meant that the social psychologist 'is inevitably part of what he or she is studying' (Sherif 1976: 362). The personal aspect was also evident in her attempts to bring students into the discipline. In her preface she wrote:

> The only way that I could translate my aims into this book was to regard the challenge as personal. In writing, I am very much there in first-person singular ... I've not hesitated to bring up controversial issues that will continue to be important or to pass my own judgments about them. Here the first person singular may be a distinct advantage for the reader. It should be easier to take issue with my personal statement than with a judgment rendered implicitly through impersonal discourse or attributed to a mythical collective wisdom.
>
> (Sherif 1976: xii–xiii)

C.W. Sherif wrote a candid comparison to her previous textbook, co-authored with her husband and colleague, Muzafer Sherif (Sherif and Sherif 1969) that reflected their differences in approach. About writing in the first person, she said, 'The experience was at times disturbing to someone like me, accustomed to writing impersonal journal articles and books, often behind the doubly protected façade of co-authorship with M. Sherif' (Sherif 1976: xii). Of the 1976 text, she informed us that it was written 'without the invaluable guiding hand of the senior author of her earlier work' and further noted, 'He did his best to persuade me to excise from the manuscript the personal context for his work. Unfortunately, I could not do so without severing part of the first-person singular from my narrative' (Sherif 1976: xiii).

C.W. Sherif observed that 'There is a strong tendency in social psychology to concentrate on stability, regularity and continuity in social behavior' (Sherif 1976: 362) and that investigative methods derive from this search for regularities. It is often personally disturbing to the social psychologist when 'social change exceeds the bounds of what social psychologists' own self-system and reference groups define as "normal" or "desirable"' (Sherif 1976: 362). The dilemma for social psychology, she said, was that 'There can be no valid laws or principles about social behavior that do not accommodate change as well as stability and continuity in social behavior' (Sherif 1976: 362–3). Her analysis of social movements – a field noticeably absent from social psychology text-books of the 1980s – was a compelling call to use these movements as laboratories for researching social change. Interestingly, research methodology was woven throughout her textbook, about which she said:

> Out of context, issues of research methods can easily appear to be nit-pickings, or worse yet 'technical matters' of concern only to tech-nicians. They come alive within their proper contexts, which are efforts by human beings to inquire into mysteries and significant issues of the human condition . . .
>
> (Sherif 1976: xii)

Through a dialogue with the reader, this text reflects something closer to the historical conception of science with its emphasis on social change, its description of the cultural and historical contexts for research studies and its insistence that social psychology and the social psychologist are neither value-free nor value-neutral.

To present social psychology within a natural science framework requires that it be written not as the personal life's work of an individual or group of individuals interested in the social world but as the most up-to-date account of 'the latest findings' and 'breakthroughs' on given topics. Research studies are reported for their significant findings and decontextualized from the researcher's sociocultural background and from the history of the field itself. What creates the illusion of a coherent and 'real' scientific social psychology is a set of standardized topics and a central commitment to reporting the latest experiments on these topics.

To present social psychology within an historical framework requires teaching from a perspective that acknowledges a broader field of social enquiry to which social psychology belongs and to locate social psychology in its diverse practices around the world and at different historical moments. In this regard, it is a useful starting place to compare textbooks and 'histories' of social psychology according to how they have constructed the discipline. Where and when did contemporary American social psychology originate? Out of what political, economic and cultural context? Historical research examines both the continuities and disconti-nuities in social theorizing and investigative practices, looking at what has fallen by the wayside and what has been systematically suppressed (Danziger 1990). Historical research examines how social psychology has developed in other parts of the world (Moghaddam 1987; Strickland 1991) and within the context of national disciplinary infrastructures (Hilgard 1987). Within an historical framework we are more likely to uncover the cultural, economic and political assumptions in our work and the implications these have for social action. Our work is more likely to become inclusive of epistemic differences to the extent that we can become less preoccupied with our identities as 'real' scientists.

Chapter 2

Kitty Genovese and culturally embedded theorizing[1]

Facts are not pure and unsullied bits of information; culture also influences what we see and how we see it. Theories, moreover, are not inexorable inductions from facts. The most creative theories are often imaginative visions imposed upon facts; the source of imagination is also strongly cultural.

(Gould 1981: 22)

It has not been common in social psychology to think of theorizing as an occasion for cultural or historical analysis. Social psychology as practised within the discipline of psychology has for several decades presented the social psychologist as a stereotypically isolated scientist at work in the laboratory searching for the laws of social behaviour that transcend cultural and historical circumstances. The main task of theorizing is presented as a cognitive one.

I learned the practice of social psychologizing in a more sociopolitical milieu – around my grandparents' dinner table. Adults speculated on the causes of world tensions and interpersonal conflicts, and voiced their solutions to both types of problems. The world of the interpersonal was continually and unashamedly juxtaposed with larger social collectivities – groups, organizations and even nations. Theorizing 'the social' and solving social problems were conjoined in my earliest recollections. As time progressed, I added in my own accountings and theorizings about events that concerned me.

Often, I think this early training at the dinner table in 'accounting for' and 'making sense of' was the kind of pre-theorizing activity that made social psychology attractive to me. As an undergraduate student in the 1960s and reading the kind of work social psychologists do, I took the field to be largely preoccupied with understanding social interaction between people and among groups. As I moved on to graduate school, the academic dinner table demanded that I become more experimental, more analytical and precise in my attempts to make sense of social situations. Graduate school 'theorizing' made my family's 'opinionizing' seem rather amateurish. For a time, the better goal seemed to be to set aside trying to account for things that concerned me personally. I was encouraged to make my 'subjects' the 'objects' of my study, to step back from the 'real' world and account for a narrower band of individual behaviour that happens in a usually narrower space/time world called a laboratory. At a later point in my life as a social psychology professor, my family's dinner table theorizing made a comeback and, combined with some of the more sensible demands of scholarship, conspired to return me to the task of making sense in morally, politically, and culturally grounded ways.

When I reflect on how I generate hunches or come up with explanations for contemporary events I am often aware of the boundedness imposed by my experiences thus far. Often I can see the assumptive framework in the family that shaped me, the larger society that shaped my family, the educational system in which I learned, the books I've read, the communities and countries I've lived in and the people with whom I've shared my life. Construed this way, I am unable to think of the social scientist as an isolated individual with sound and rational private abstractions about cultural experience. Rather, the social scientist appears to me as a passionate and public person. As one such person, the social psychologist constructs an understanding of the social world that she or he inhabits. An imagined line is broken between the past and the present, between 'historical research' and 'social science research'. Social psychology becomes a powerful post-dictive science of meaning more than a predictive science of control based on the model of the physical sciences.[2] Generating hypotheses about social situations involves constructing meaning from one's own cultural experience, sharing that meaning publicly, and finding tension and conflict with other points of view through public discussion and enquiry. It necessitates more than one understanding of the same event and exposes the difficulty of resolving conflicting viewpoints.

The link between an historical event and the social and political practice of theorizing about it that engages me as a social psychologist can be illustrated by my discipline's account of bystander intervention. Through introductory social psychology textbooks most North American students of social psychology have become familiar with the murder in 1964 of Catherine (Kitty) Genovese in Queens, New York. We have learned to think of this event as an instance of the failure of bystanders to intervene in emergency situations. Our contact with the event has for three decades been shaped by the social psychological research of Bibb Latané and John Darley, who both graduated with PhDs in 1964 and 1965 respectively. They were responding to the event in 1964 and to numerous headlines, many of which reported the incident as an instance of 'apathy': 'Apathy at stabbing of Queens woman shocks inspector' (*New York Times*: 27 March 1964); 'Apathy is puzzle in Queens killing' (*NYT*: 28 March 1964).

In a later interview with Rand Evans (1980), Darley described their thinking. 'Latané and I, shocked as anybody else, met over dinner a few days after this terrible incident had occurred and began to analyze this process in social psychological terms . . .' (Evans 1980: 216). These researchers were not satisfied to think of the event in terms of the 'personality' characteristics of the onlookers, such as apathy, or to set the event in the context of social norms. Instead, they explained the passivity of the onlookers to this murder by using theoretical concepts that focused on immediate situational factors that might inhibit helping in emergencies. Concepts of group-inhibition and diffusion of responsibility in large groups were invoked and became the focus of later empirical work.

At the time, others made sense of the event differently. On 27 March 1964, a lengthy piece appeared in the *New York Times* (*NYT*). The main headline read '37 who saw murder didn't call the police'. A *Times* editorial on 28 March asked, 'Who can explain such shocking indifference on the part of a cross-section of our fellow New Yorkers?' and answered, 'We regretfully admit that we do not know the answers'. 'Behavioral specialists hard put to explain witnesses' failure to call police' none the less offered their analyses (*NYT*: 28 March 1964). A police commissioner thought that 'this tendency to shy away from reporting crimes is a common one', while a lawyer wanted a 'Law Day' held throughout the United States to 'fight this tendency to look the other way' and to 'indoctrinate the public with their responsibility'. One sociologist commented on how our inability to defend each other brings us close to being 'partners in crime'. Another sociologist likened the reaction of the witnesses to a 'disaster syndrome' as if one witnessed a tornado. One psychiatrist assigned blame to living in a big city that alienates the individual from the group. Another psychiatrist saw it as typical middle-class behaviour in a city like New York where people 'have a nice life and what happens in the street, the life of the city itself, is a different matter', further warning that action might lead to one's own victimization. One reverend noted that his society 'is as sick as the one that crucified Jesus' and another reverend talked of the parable of the Good Samaritan. In a later article, another psychiatrist suggested that 'the murder vicariously gratified the sadistic impulses of those who witnessed it' (*NYT*: 12 April 1964). Each commentator constructed his version of the incident within the framework that he had chosen to interpret life, chosen to answer the essential questions of theorizing: What's going on here? Why is this happening? What is it about?

In the *Letter to the Times* section of the *New York Times* that followed from 31 March to 24 May, numerous attempts to find a meaningful way to interpret this event were submitted. These constructions represented diverse views: there was a failure of morality at its worst in large cities; people were immersed in themselves; they were apathetic, much as the

Germans were to the plight of the Jews; there was a fear of police reprisal; a failure of the American male to do the manly and courageous thing; what could one expect with so much violence in the mass media? What better argument for keeping weapons in one's house! On 3 May 1964 A.M. Rosenthal, then Metropolitan editor for the *New York Times*, wrote a lengthier analysis for the *New York Times Magazine* (*NYTM*) focusing on the apathy of the bystanders, but noting also that

> Each individual obviously approaches the story of Catherine Genovese, reacts to it and veers away from it against the background of his own life experience, and his own fears and shortcomings and rationalizations.
>
> (Rosenthal, in *NYTM* 1964: 69)

A professional identification with experimental social psychology carries with it a strong tendency towards behavioural and situational explanations. Not surprisingly, the analysis offered by Latané and Darley in the 1960s was a theoretical construction based on the immediate situational determinants of behaviours such as noticing, judging and taking personal responsibility through action. An inverse relationship between group size and helping behaviour figured prominently in their empirical work, and reflected a longstanding preoccupation with social psychology defined as the influence of people in one another's lives (Latané and Darley 1970). However, by moving in as closely as possible to the behavioural phenomenon and casting the event in terms of independent variables such as size of group that affect dependent variables such as intervening behaviour, these researchers chose to 'veer away' from a sociocultural analysis of the event.

Here's how I think theorizing happens. During an initial period of reflection, the social psychologist, like other members of society, asks him/herself and others, 'Did you see the headlines?' 'Did you read about Kitty Genovese?' 'So what was that about?' 'Why did that happen?' In addition, the academic theorizer is subtly guided by his or her socialization into a discipline's normative beliefs about appropriate intellectual frameworks and scientifically respectable methodologies for bringing together hunch and evidence.[3] It is in this effort to *construct* the meaning of an event where we also *constrict* our vision, where we fail to ask the question, 'Of what else is this event an instance?' Here is where 'normal science' begins, where Kitty Genovese's murder becomes an instance of a seemingly larger category of social behaviour designated as 'bystander intervention'.

Consider for a moment that Kitty Genovese and her assailant, Winston Moseley, were living in a society at a time when its members did little to intervene in violence directed towards women. Such details were not the central part of the abstraction/construction process by which 'general processes' of social behaviour were hypothesized and later empirically tested. In the mid-1960s, what was abstracted as the general phenomenon of interest was something like this: there was an emergency and no one intervened to help.

As a graduate student in the early 1970s, in the heyday of bystander intervention research and at the pre-dawning of my own feminist consciousness, I can't claim to have seen anything other than Latané and Darley's point of view. Only later, while reviewing literature relevant to the social psychology of rape (Cherry 1983), did I come across information that shifted the context for the event and altered my framework for thinking about the meaning of Kitty Genovese's death.[4]

The murder of Kitty Genovese in 1964 was described in detail by Susan Brownmiller in her book on rape, *Against Our Will* (1975). Brownmiller was writing about known rapists who continued unchecked by police, and to her the 'event' symbolized something quite different from the inaction of bystanders:

> It comes as a surprise to most people that the murder of Kitty Genovese, stalked and stabbed to death shortly after 3 a.m. on a bleak commercial-residential street in Queens on March 13, 1964 – a much discussed case in the nineteen sixties because thirty-eight people heard the victim's cries or witnessed some part of her ordeal without calling the police – ended in her rape as she lay dying. Winston Moseley, Genovese's 29-year-old killer, later made an extraordinary confession. 'I just set out to find any girl that was unattended and I was going to kill her,' he calmly announced in court.
>
> (Brownmiller 1975: 199)

Brownmiller, writing in the mid-1970s for a North American audience becoming increasingly vocal about violence towards women, called attention to the 'stubborn particulars' of gender implicated in this incident. By the 1980s, my thinking about this incident might be better expressed this way: violence was directed at yet another woman by a man and no one intervened to help her. What has changed over the years is the way I name the incident as well as the cultural framework in which the incident is reinterpreted.

In early accounts, only one onlooker was reported to have expressed a reluctance to intervene in what might have been a 'lovers' quarrel' (Rosenthal 1964), thereby specifying something gendered about the meaning of the situation. In fact, what followed this incident at the time were the numerous experimental simulations of generalized bystander behaviour in emergency situations: hearing someone having an epileptic seizure and reporting it; reporting a room filling with smoke; coming to the aid of a woman in distress as she is heard to fall and apparently hurt herself. None of these simulations involved situations of attack.

However, all were excellent examples of how research can strip meaning from events at the creative phase of theorizing about the world. Sex/ gender violence was excluded at the phase of abstracting hypotheses about social reality. The link to the Kitty Genovese incident was stripped of its original gendered particulars, that is, an *attack* on a woman was no longer an essential component in the laboratory exploration of what the event meant.

This is not surprising given that in 1964 we lived in a world that did not recognize by name the widespread abuse of women. Feminist movement throughout the 1970s 'enlarged our definition of violence to take in abuse of children, and the discussion of rape, spousal abuse, incest and pornography, clitorectomy' (Apfelbaum and Lubek 1983). The increasing momentum of the women's movement to confront violence in the 1970s allowed for a different framework for my understanding of the murder of Kitty Genovese. This shift in framework was part of a larger ongoing shift to view social psychology as an interpretive rather than predictive science. In my own training as an experimental social psychologist, I was urged to conceptualize my understanding of events in terms of 'variables' rather than 'persons'.[5] I would more easily ask the question – 'Is sex of subject a significant variable in my multivariate analysis of helping behaviour?' than 'What is this about for people particularized with respect to their sex, race and class, namely those aspects of persons which form the material and psychological experience of the world?' I remember being trained to think that it is more elegant to strip questions of their social embeddedness, such that 'bystander behaviour' is considered scientifically purer than what you can learn from trying to make sense of the specifics of the murder/rape of a woman. However, my own experiences with the women's movement and my own feminist politicization prevented me from seeing this event exclusively within the framework of unresponsive bystander intervening behaviour. Rather, I found myself returning to view Genovese's murder first within the framework of sex/gender relationships and then within an even larger framework of multiple structures of powerlessness (sex, race, age and class) that play themselves out in our daily lives.

As my perspective shifted, I began to take more seriously the view of social psychology as a science that thrives within historical and cultural contexts and with that my views on experimentation were also altered. I found it difficult to believe that there were critical experiments rather than just historically important ones that foster a greater understanding of the world we live in. Social experiments are not crucial tests of the truth of competing hypotheses but reflect the experimenter's cultural knowledge by locating an appropriate social context for displaying that knowledge (Gergen 1978). Given this approach, understanding and insight will be augmented by research that does not decontextualize social phenomena, but rather attempts to address the social context in which phenomena are located.

There were two such experimental studies in social psychology that I kept for a long time in a file folder marked 'these mean something'. The two studies were conceptual anomalies in the unresponsive bystander literature which later allowed me to see how social context informs hypothesis generation. The studies did not decontextualize the Genovese incident but rather viewed her plight as an aspect of generalized sex-role reactions to women under attack. In the first study Borofsky *et al.* (1971) conducted a role-playing experiment with male and female dyads where an attack was simulated. They found that none of six male observers tried to stop a man assaulting a woman while in other dyads, male helping was at a higher rate. Women were unlikely to intervene in any of the four role-played dyads, a finding that received no explanation. The researchers explained the male behaviour by the possible 'vicarious sexual and/or hostile gratification from seeing a man injure a woman' (Borofsky *et al.* 1971: 317). It was too early for this study to become an overnight classic spawning further research on the general question of unimpeded violence towards women.

A second study, by Shotland and Straw, appeared in 1976, at a time when feminist activism was becoming increasingly focused on collective intervention in the form of rape crisis centres and homes for battered wives run by women. The authors conducted a rather elaborate set of experiments to examine more carefully the Genovese attack as it occurred in its original context. In their study of staged assaults and reactions to these assaults they found that 'intervention occurred much more frequently when subjects perceived the attacker and victim as strangers (65%) rather than married (19%)' (Shotland and Straw 1976: 992), and subjects were more likely to infer an intimate connection between the man and woman when they were unsure about the relationship. In the 1960s, bystander behaviour was the general phenomenon of which sex-paired dyads were a subcase. In the 1980s, gender-role expectations became the general phenomenon and bystander behaviour became a subcase.

Shotland and Straw ended their research by making a plea for knowing one's neighbours as a way of reducing faulty inferences and as a means of facilitating 'social control' in the community. They were operating on the assumption that violence (rape included) is largely a phenomenon between strangers, which we now know is not the case. They concluded: 'If we could obtain this control in terms of a man beating up a woman, we might be able to restrict the victimization of women to their husbands or close associates' (Shotland and Straw 1976: 999), acknowledging in a footnote that 'If bystanders and, one would guess, society do not regard wife beating seriously, this act cannot be controlled' (Shotland and Straw 1976: 999). It should be remembered that these authors were writing at a time when the extent of wife battering was not well documented, when a wife could not legally claim to have been raped and when violence against women was interpreted from the perspective of psychopathology of either the offender or the victim. Despite such limitations, the two studies managed to produce an experimental analogue for another interpretation of the original Kitty Genovese incident.

These two anomalous studies were not focused on bystander apathy or diffusion of responsibility as the major theoretical explanation but on the nature and perception of male–female relatedness. Despite all the training to see the world in gender-neutral terms, these two studies were early evidence that some researchers could not ignore what was going on around them, namely, an increasing awareness of the prevalence of violence towards women. A footnote in the Shotland and Straw study bears this out. Describing the social milieu on the campus on which the study was conducted in 1974, Shotland and Straw stated that 'approximately six to nine months prior to the experiment there were a number of assaults, on campus and in town, on women, of both a sexual and non-sexual nature. The attacks had caused much concern and a great deal of publicity' (Shotland and Straw 1976: 991). These two studies[6] form a bridge between understanding Genovese's murder in terms of the unresponsive bystander paradigm and understanding it in the context of changing sex/gender relations.

If theorizing is an historically situated activity, it becomes dangerous to canonize events and the research that follows as having one meaning for all time. Over the course of a decade, the 'Genovese incident' changed for me from being about the behavioural problem of bystanders failing to intervene in emergencies to being about the social problem of violence towards women. In summarizing ten years of research on group size and helping behaviour, Latané and Nida asked:

> After 10 years and over 50 studies, what can be concluded? . . . [T]he original phenomenon discovered by Latané and Darley has a firm empirical foundation and has withstood the tests of time and replication. Although we have not discussed it in this review, the research has also led to interesting theoretical advances . . . To our knowledge, however, the research has not contributed to the development of practical strategies for increasing bystander intervention. Although the original experiments and the continuing interest in the topic were certainly stimulated, at least in part, by the dramatic, real-world case of the failure of 38 witnesses to intervene in or even report to the police the murder of Kitty Genovese, not one of us has been able to mobilize the increasing store of social psychological understanding accumulated over the last decade to devise suggestions for ensuring that future Kitty Genoveses will receive help.
>
> (Latané and Nida 1981: 322)

Their lack of finding practical strategies within the bystander paradigm for 'ensuring that future Kitty Genoveses will receive help' needs to be reconceptualized in the context of the past twenty-five years of the legal, medical and social-psychological support network operated by women that includes rape awareness campaigns, rape crisis centres, transition homes for battered women and more.

At some point, I began to reconsider that Genovese's murder, while an instance of violence towards women, had still broader implications. It signalled a growing expression of a community's sense of powerlessness to prevent violence. Increased reporting of attacks on women also seemed to indicate that some communities were more vulnerable than others, because of race and social class. I became curious to discover whether race or class were ever presented as part of the understanding of Genovese's murder. I turned back to the press coverage in the *New York Times* that covered the initial murder-rape and has continued to discuss it.[7] I systematically traced each reference to Genovese and/or Moseley in the *New York Times* from 1964 to 1988, including Letters to the Editor, editorial opinions and special comments in the *Times Supplement*. The original report of the murder of Catherine Genovese appeared on 14 March 1964, with the headline 'Queens woman is stabbed to death in front of home'. In the course of this analysis, the contexts of gender, race and class emerged at different points to provide an understanding of the event as part of a more complex picture of violence in American communities than could be revealed in laboratory studies of bystander intervention.

The story of the murder did not end with a brief one-column report but accelerated when an in-depth investigation revealed that thirty-eight onlookers (safe in the privacy of their own apartments) failed to intervene even by contacting the police. Rosenthal subsequently interviewed witnesses and other professionals, and he quite candidly described the race and class dimensions of victimization that affected the very way in which the story was constructed. He wrote in his book, *Thirty-Eight Witnesses*:

> The truth also is that if Miss Genovese had been killed on Park Avenue or Madison Avenue an assistant would have called the story to my attention, I would have assigned a top man and quite possibly we would have had a front-page story the next morning. If she had been a white woman killed in Harlem, the tension of the integration story would have provided her with a larger obituary. If she had been a Negro killed in Harlem she would have received a paragraph or two.
>
> (Rosenthal 1964: 16)

We know about Catherine Genovese partly because she was a white woman killed in a predominantly middle-class neighbourhood, and no one intervened to help her. As for the assailant, Rosenthal wrote further that 'during the life of the story we received a few nasty letters demanding to know why we had "concealed" the fact that Moseley was Negro. The answer is really quite simple. Where the fact that a man is a Negro is directly relevant to the story we print the fact. Where it is not, we do not' (Rosenthal 1964: 18–19). In his testimony, Moseley indicated that he went out looking for 'any girl' and the *New York Times* coverage made little of his actions as racially motivated.[8] More was made of how such a thing could have happened in a middle-class neighbourhood.

In all the social psychological experimentation that followed the focus shifted to the bystanders, away from the victim and the assailant. At the time of the murder and subsequent trial, Moseley was in his late twenties. He was married to a registered nurse and they had two children. He worked as a business-machine operator. Other details emerged as I traced what happened to Moseley through the press coverage in the *New York Times*. His lawyer's opening remarks 'dwelt in some detail on the frustrations of his client's early years in Detroit and Pittsburgh, describing him as an "intelligent, quiet, shy, retiring boy" who somehow developed from an introvert into a maniac' (*NYT*: 9 June 1964). We learn that his crime was painstakingly calculated, that he confessed to and subsequently recanted the murders of two other women. Brownmiller, in her analysis some years later, described him as one of the 'fairly typical, if unusually dramatic examples of the men who commit rape-murder . . . better understood as brutalized, violence-prone men who act out their raging hatred against the world through an object offering the least amount of physical resistance, a woman's body' (Brownmiller 1975: 206).

Winston Moseley was found guilty of murder in the first degree and sentenced to the electric chair amidst handclapping and the cheers of women in the courtroom. The judge told the jurors that he didn't believe in capital punishment, but added this note, 'I must say I feel this may be improper when I see this monster. I wouldn't hesitate to pull the switch on him myself' (*NYT*: 16 June 1964). During the trial the prosecution introduced evidence of other women's encounters with Moseley that included physical and sexual assault. He entered Sing Sing Prison in July 1964 to await execution, which was delayed by the appeal process. That process resulted on 1 June 1967 in a reduction of his sentence to life imprisonment. He had been considered legally sane for the purposes of being tried but was still suffering from mental illness which the court ruled, 'while not a defense to the crime, may have rendered it impossible for him to exercise any self-control' (*People v. Moseley* 1967: 765; see note 7, pp. 115–16). The appeal acknowledged his legal sanity but argued that mental illness should have played a role in sentencing. In 1965, the State of New York had abolished the death penalty and

Moseley had already been advised that his sentence would become life imprisonment.

Moseley was transferred to Attica State Prison and in 1968 was taken to Meyer Memorial Hospital in Buffalo for minor surgery. He escaped while being taken back to Attica and was considered dangerous. The press coverage in the *New York Times* from 19 March to 23 April reminded readers repeatedly of his earlier offense and he was eventually captured by the FBI, arraigned for rape, burglary, robbery, unlawful escape and unlawful possession of a firearm and returned to Attica State Prison.

In the course of involving several people in his escape, a black woman was held hostage and raped. *She* was later charged with aiding his escape. She did not report his hiding place because he threatened to kill her children if she told. Despite her own victimization by Moseley, she could have received a year in prison. The case was dismissed but not before Mrs Barbara Sims, the only black woman lawyer on the prosecuting staff, refused to prosecute the case and was quoted as saying 'If this had been a white woman raped, do you think they would have brought her into court and charged her with a crime?' (*NYT*: 3 April 1968). Sims was dismissed for insubordination. These events of 1968 were only a small part of the racial turmoil in many American black communities anguished further by the assassination of Martin Luther King Jr on 4 April 1968.

Does it end there with Moseley going back to jail? Actually not. On 16 April 1977, an editorial written by Winston Moseley appeared in the *New York Times*. The letter bears out earlier information that Moseley was intelligent and expressed himself well. At his trial, he had said that murder was an idea that came into his mind and that he could not put it aside. One defence psychiatrist had labelled him catatonic schizophrenic, 'incapable of stopping himself once he got the urge to kill', and another defence psychiatrist said he 'knew enough to take escape measures but that otherwise defects of reason had severely impaired his judgement', and in rebuttal another psychiatrist believed he was aware of the wrong-doing of his actions, showing 'good logic, judgement and intelligence in carrying out his plans' (*NYT*: 11 June 1964).

In his editorial Winston Moseley describes his life. In 1971, he was part of the Attica prison uprising, an experience that he says accounts for the beginning of his learning 'that human life has great value'. He earned a BA degree in sociology when courses were offered in prison. He cites two women, Sister Mary Frances Welch and Dorothy Tishler, who assisted him in a personal transformation. He has been president and vice-president of the inmate liaison committee of Attica and assisted in prison reform and a peaceful demonstration at Attica in 1977. He tells us 'The man who killed Kitty Genovese in Queens in 1964 is no more' (*NYT*: 16 April 1977).

On 28 April 1977, two letters to the editor of the *New York Times* appeared with the heading 'Convict rehabilitation: unconvincing evidence'. In one, the writer argues that murder is not a rational crime and Moseley's education and greater social awareness hardly convince her that he is rehabilitated. She says 'Mr. Moseley should demonstrate that those factors in his personality which motivated him to kill Kitty Genovese will not reassert themselves'. Another writes:

> The Moseley article? Proof that writing can be taught. I would feel much safer if I were sure that some do-gooder doesn't try to get him out of Attica. The Kitty Genovese murder will continue to haunt us all.
>
> (*NYT*: 28 April 1977)

Indeed, this particular historical event will continue to raise questions about how we are to prevent violence towards women. However, if we stay too focused on violence towards women, we lose sight of other systemic factors that structure violence – poverty, race and class. While not absolving Moseley of his crime, we still need to understand the world that formed him in his 'early years in Detroit and Pittsburgh' in the 1930s and 1940s. Furthermore, the 'commitment to anti-sexist and anti-racist work' (hooks 1990: 64) requires that we are always looking at the political context of the crime despite our outrage at the victimizers. The daily experience of violence in people's lives is a story too easily decontextualized by social psychological theories that operate at the individual behavioural level. If we theorize at the level of community, then we begin to consider that some groups or communities are more vulnerable to violence than others and have been so historically. By understanding the overlap of racism, sexism and poverty, we can understand both the personal suffering and the political significance of any particular attack. Theorizing about the Genovese incident involves us in theorizing about the relative power or powerlessness of groups and communities to protect themselves from violence. This theme slowly emerged through the 1980s and was reflected in some of the later commentary on the Genovese murder.

Maureen Dowd, in a piece entitled '20 years after the murder of Kitty Genovese – the question remains: Why?', wrote that this murder 'crystallized what people were only beginning to feel about urban life in America: the anonymity, the lack of human contact, the feeling of not being able to control one's environment' (*NYT*: 12 March 1984). Indeed, the incident occurred before American national crime rates soared. Dowd reported on views put forward at a Catherine Genovese Memorial Conference at Fordham University marking the twentieth anniversary of Genovese's murder. In the opinion of a university administrator:

> Kitty Genovese died because we didn't have a sense of community. We're finally coming out of it now because people are tired of being afraid to walk on the streets or go in the subways.
>
> (Sexter, in Dowd *NYT* 12 March 1984)

And of subsequent incidents, the conference was told by the then Surgeon General of the United States that they would decline:

> [W]hen people learn to care, when they accept the fact that there may be risks to caring, and when they agree to take those risks in order to preserve their place in the community.
>
> (Koop, in Dowd *NYT* 12 March 1984)

The speaker claimed that risks are required to preserve 'community' but one wants to ask whose community will be preserved? Since 1964 several stories have been reported in the *New York Times* that were reminiscent of the Genovese incident. By the mid-1980s, a magazine editor, L.J. Davis, living nearby the scene of another woman's murder lamented that 'fights – violent, destructive fights, often accompanied by the display if not the use of murderous hardware – are roughly as common as trips to the post office. The wonder, therefore, is not that many people failed to summon the police; the wonder is that anybody bothered' (*NYT*: 19 December 1984); and that poorer communities were more vulnerable: 'everyone knows what happens when you lock a sane man up in a madhouse. . . . Until we address the reality of the poor, they will remain locked in the same hermetic and unbroken cycle of rage, and sometimes they will kill each other' (*NYT*: 19 December 1984).

Rosenthal, whose accounts of the Genovese murder and the police's response to crime were cited earlier, wrote an article entitled 'The 39th witness' (*NYT*: 12 February 1987). He described his reaction to New York City's homeless, perhaps the most powerless community of all:

> I hoped that I would never be a silent witness. . . . Almost every day of my life I see a body sprawled on the sidewalk. . . . They do not scream, as did Catherine Genovese, but if they did I would probably walk even faster, because they are dirty, sometimes foul persons, a most unattractive and unsympathetic kind of victim. . . . Sometimes I get very angry. . . . Then, sometimes and more often recently, I think of Catherine Genovese and the way she died and the 38 witnesses. I check out a little book I wrote about the case then and find that I didn't really attack the 38 and wrote that any one of us might have done the same. I am glad I was not too high and mighty about them because now I am the 39th. And whether you live in New York or any other city where living bodies lie in the streets or roam them in pain, and walk by, so are you.
>
> (Rosenthal in *NYT*: 12 February 1987)

When we theorize about violence in communities, it is important to look at how understanding and experience are structured by the material conditions of poverty and systemic exclusion from power. Intervening or turning away are behaviours best understood in historical and cultural context. The circumstances of Genovese's murder that I originally understood in individual behavioural terms became, during the 1970s, an instance of the general failure to intervene in the prevention of violence towards women. Now I use that incident as a springboard to understand how whole communities can be seen as vulnerable to unchecked violence. I think it is the task of social psychology to theorize a sociopolitics of intervention starting with increased knowledge of the long and complex history of non-intervention in instances of violence against powerless groups – women, the aged, children, racial minorities and the poor, among others.

Chapter 3

Struggling with theory and theoretical struggles[1]

An appropriately poignant image of the knower (and especially of the theorist) is that of a rope walker who, on arriving at a precipice of ignorance, ties one end of a chain of inferences to a stake on its brink, and flinging the free end as far as possible out over the abyss, runs quickly along the thrown chain to get the maximum distance before plunging to disaster. Limited knowledge representations being all we have, the only thing worse than generating and using them is not doing so.

(McGuire 1983)

On 14 December 1989 in the late afternoon, the media reported that Marc Lepine, a man in his early twenties, had murdered fourteen women at the *École polytechnique*, the engineering school of the University of Montreal. At the end of his shooting spree, he killed himself. As more of the details of that afternoon were released, news commentators were preoccupied with questions of motive. For many in the feminist community, the answer was horrifyingly clear: Lepine had made a political statement that pushed violence against women to its ultimate expression – mass murder. What feminists encountered after the event was the backlash that arises when an act of male violence towards an individual woman is viewed as an action with political dimensions, that is, an action against women collectively. In the field of social psychology, Ken Gergen has used the term 'generative theorizing' to capture something of the struggle that I would argue took place when feminists challenged individualistic accounts of Marc Lepine's actions. Gergen has described generative theorizing in the following way:

It may be useful, then, to consider competing theoretical accounts in terms of their generative capacity, that is, the capacity to challenge the guiding assumptions of the culture, to raise fundamental questions regarding contemporary social life, to foster reconsideration of that which is 'taken for granted', and thereby to furnish new alternatives for social action. It is the generative theory that can provoke debate, transform social reality, and ultimately serve to reorder social conduct.

(Gergen 1978: 1346)

We now know that Marc Lepine had intended to kill prominent feminists. One of them, journalist Francine Pelletier, released a part of his suicide note that in Lepine's own words crystallized the political link between gender and aggression in his troubled mind:

Please note that if I commit suicide today . . . it is not for economic reasons . . . but for political reasons. For I have decided to send [to the death] the feminists who have always ruined my life, to their Maker. . . . Even if the Mad Killer epithet will be attributed to me by the media, I consider myself a rational erudite [person]. . . . Being rather backward-looking by nature [except for science], the feminists always have a talent to enrage me. They want to keep the advantages of women [e.g. cheaper insurance, extended maternity leave preceded by a preventive retreat etc.] while trying to grab those of the men.

(*Toronto Globe and Mail*: 27 November 1990)

The full note was followed by a 'hit list' of the names of nineteen women with the added comment: 'Nearly died today. The lack of time (because I started too late) has allowed those radical feminists to survive'. Instead of murdering high-profile feminist activists, Lepine acted against women engineering students whose inroads into a male-dominated world might just as easily have fed his rage.[2] In one lecture hall filled with male and female students, he shouted, 'Women to one side. You are all feminists. I hate feminists.' One survivor reported how she attempted to reason with him by saying, 'We are only women in engineering who want to live a normal life' (Lakeman 1990: 20).

In the days that followed the massacre, feminist activist Lee Lakeman (1990) analysed the news media's tendency to avoid viewing Lepine's actions as an expression of male violence towards women and the women's movement. The Canadian news media individualized Lepine's actions and portrayed him as a madman acting out a brutal scenario. Lakeman described how women across Canada mobilized vigils and resisted the media's attempts to present women as overreacting. Her analysis did not gloss over the differences in women's political understanding of the crime. She documented the words of one woman who came to mourn because 'the murder of any woman is a reason to organize' whereas other women stayed away 'vowing that, until the murder of poor women, native women, runaways and prostitutes causes public outcry, they will put their energy elsewhere' (Lakeman 1990: 22).

One year later, the polarization of feeling around the deaths of the Montreal women and the meaning of Lepine's actions remained. The term 'chilly climate' has been increasingly used to describe the atmosphere at Canadian universities. Shortly after the murders in 1989, for example, a poster with lace and roses in the background appeared across many Canadian university campuses. The text reads:

> 14 women died
> in Montreal
> December 6, 1989.
> 97 women died
> in domestic violence
> in 1988 in Canada.
> First mourn.
> Then work for change.

Almost one year later, at my university, a copy of the poster was found defaced. Someone had drawn the scope of a gun in the centre of the poster and bullet holes in two other places. Dave Naylor, then editor-in-chief of the Carleton student newspaper, *The Charlatan*, reflected on the significance of this action:

> The 'artist', no doubt a male, obviously wants to send a message to women. The message? that there are lots more Marc Lepines out there, and there is a little bit of Marc Lepine in all men. I don't happen to believe this is true. . . . I think almost every male hates Marc Lepine for what he did to the relationships between sexes, as well as for his atrocities against humanity. No male wants to be represented even in the slightest way by such a horrifying symbol. . . . How can women be convinced Marc Lepine is not in any way representative of males? How can we express our compassion for the loss of women's lives?
>
> (Naylor 1990: 12)

This passage raises many questions that challenge the 'taken for granted' view that Marc Lepine's actions are best understood as 'madness'. In fact, by asking 'Is there a little bit of him in all men?' an analytical framework is generated that contextualizes Lepine's actions in the study of men's daily lives and the cultural construction of masculinity. In my view, feminist theorizing over the past twenty-five years has shifted our understanding to a point where this question among others becomes quite important. Who are the men who identify with Lepine? Who are the men who oppose him by working towards equality for women in their personal and political lives? Feminist theorizing over the past twenty-five years has shifted our understanding to a point where we can now ask these new questions about men and masculinity.

Traditionally, when the question of why men violate women's bodies and lives were asked, the answers given were individualized and blame was located with women themselves. Psychological theories of violence towards women operating at this individualized level of analysis often left women doubly victimized. However, theorizing male violence towards women has evolved over the past twenty-five years since the late 1960s when feminists began a systematic study of rape. Before then, rape was studied from a perspective of individual psychology and mental health; it was seen as sexually motivated and female-precipitated (Albin 1977). This perspective was bolstered by psychoanalytic writings, by studies of the psychopathology of incarcerated rapists, and by the new field of victimology (Clark and Lewis 1977). Susan Schechter (1982) has described a similar history of theories for explaining wife-battering.

Throughout the 1970s to the present, many feminist researchers developed their work alongside or outside of mainstream social psychological thinking and research. This was only partially a result of the omission of women as subjects or targets in the experimental analogues of social psychological research on interpersonal aggression (Frodi *et al.* 1977). I would argue that mainstream social psychology simply did not tell us what we needed and wanted to know.

More fully, there are several reasons why I think some feminist researchers did not pursue the idea of adding women to the highly stylized aggression paradigms they encountered in the early 1970s.[3] First, a simple 'add women' alteration to the practice of laboratory work in social psychology would not provide detailed information about the range and commonness of experiences women have with male violence. Only listening to women who have experienced violence could yield that information. A change from laboratory to survey and interview methods better suited the knowledge required and marks a substantial shift in scientific practice among feminist researchers. Second, as detailed knowledge of women's experience accrued, the symmetry assumed by the factorial design in traditional laboratory aggression paradigms was not an accurate way to represent that knowledge. Knowledge gained from talking with women challenged the idea that male violence towards women bears much in common *quantitatively* and *qualitatively* with inter-sex violence and/or female violence towards men. Third, by conducting studies that reduce the experience of violence in women's lives to a laboratory paradigm that stresses antecedent–consequent relationships, there is an implicit agreement to an investigative practice that produces generalizations about female-precipitated violence. Men's behavioural responses are further legitimated as 'natural' reactions to the provocating stimuli (Dutton 1986). Women's accounts of violence suggest that their alleged 'frustration' and 'attack' are not precipitators of violence but are the rationalizations men use after the fact of violence. Exclusive reliance on modes of inquiry that stress mechanistic thinking lessens the likelihood that male aggression involving women will be explored in the context of masculine identity and its connection to legal, political and economic privilege.

A fourth reason for not adding women to the existing laboratory paradigms has to do with the power of naming. There is a consciousness-raising process for women who try to understand instances of violence in women's lives through research. Often I think it is marked by a point where the idea that knowledge exists 'for its own sake' is challenged. Research 'for women's sake' names the phenomenon 'male violence towards women' and begins to explore the experiences of violence in women's lives. Problematizing the phenomenon as 'the experimental analysis of interpersonal aggression' provides a gender neutrality that obscures women's experience. Finally, published work on violence from a feminist perspective intentionally links with direct efforts to seek change for potential and actual victims of violence. For example, research differentiating 'founded and unfounded' rape (Clark and Lewis 1977), identifying rape trauma syndrome (Burgess and Holmstrom 1974) and battered woman syndrome (Walker 1984) grounds its generalizations in the concrete lives of women speaking out against violence. It reflects the lives of women calling rape crisis phone lines, taking their first women's self-defence course and arriving at police stations, hospitals, shelters and offices of sexual harassment advisors. In this way, conceptual and empirical work have stayed connected such that they can be useful to women's emancipation from the belief that women are responsible for male violence.

Throughout the 1970s an analysis of rape from the victim's point of view was emerging as a competing theoretical framework to previous work. Several aspects of this emergent perspective illustrate the concept of generative theorizing. First, acts of rape were contextualized not as the generalized phenomenon of 'aggression' but as an aspect of close male–female relationships. Feminist research differentiated and acknowledged rape within different types of close relationships – date-rape and marital rape – where it had previously gone unacknowledged. Second, male power and dominance in society were given a central theoretical function, undermining the analysis of rape as primarily sexually motivated. This emphasis provided an understanding of the way in which sexual aggression or the threat of it is used to maintain male power and privilege at all levels – familial, legal and economic. Theorizing rape as an expression of male power has been generalized throughout the 1980s to other cultural variants including incest, wife-battering, sexual harassment and the proliferation of violent pornography. In turn, the study of these issues has generated a reinterpretation of phenomena previously construed exclusively in the context of female pathology, namely, running away from home, prostitution, multiple personality disorder and lesbianism.

Much has been found out about women's experience as victims of male violence through first-person accounts, interviews with and surveys of survivors of abuse. These data are accepted as valid scientific evidence and mark a substantial shift in scientific practice away from a laboratory paradigm in which manipulation and control of variables are central. The shift in practice further underscores the connectedness of what is known with the methods for gathering knowledge. Detailed knowledge about women's experience cannot be separated from the narrative methods used to generate that knowledge any more than one can separate knowledge of subjects' button-pressing behaviour from the laboratory method used to generate it.

As women speak out about their experience with male violence, these acts of aggression are less often conceptualized as isolated acts of abnormality or as men's necessary response to provocation. Rather, an instance of aggression is located in a complex network of institutions – the family, the criminal justice system and the workplace. It is these larger social collectivities that give individual men licence to harm individual women with minimal consequences for doing so and it is in that framework that feminist theory as generative theory has the capacity to challenge the *status quo*. An analysis that began with research on rape has now been extended to link previously isolated phenomena such as wife-battering and incest, sexual harassment and sex discrimination. At a minimum, the framework of 'male violence towards women' has taken actions previously seen as psychologically deviant and placed them in the context of many social, political and economic interactions between men and women.

Though a feminist theory of male violence towards women has been extremely useful to those working for social change in women's lives, I often wonder whether the shift in perspective has much bearing on men's lives. Returning to the murders of the fourteen women in Montreal, Lee Lakeman documented her observations of men's reactions to women's expressions of rage and grief:

> Some men are afraid for women; some warn us to keep quiet so as not to attack the rage of other men. Some send money to the shelter and others arrange a discussion group for men to work out their defensive responses. Many seem only to be seeking our approval; instead of asking themselves and each other what they can do to change, they are asking us to take care of them.
>
> (Lakeman 1990: 22)

Harry Brod (1987) has talked about an ambivalence men might experience if feminist theory (and I would argue, real social change) requires men to examine their 'socialization towards violence'. Though violence against women continues, my impression is that there is a small but growing participation of men in the struggle against sexism and violence.[4] In my community a year after the deaths of the Montreal women, a poster appeared that speaks to men's growing activism. The poster was produced by Brother Peace, a group of men working to end male violence and it is very much in keeping with an account of violence towards women as politically constituted. The text reads:

JUSTICE

WOMEN DESERVE NO LESS   MEN DESERVE NO MORE

Women have the right to:

safety in the streets, safety in the home,
reproductive choice
be treated as equals, not objects
economic independence
challenge men without fear
love other women

Men have the responsibility to:

take 'no' for an answer
speak out against sexist behaviour
support lesbian and gay rights
share housework and the care of children
reject pornography
challenge men's anger towards feminists
listen to women

In some ways this poster answers the question posed in Dave Naylor's editorial, namely, 'How can women be convinced Marc Lepine is not in any way representative of males?' The editorial writer called for trust and cooperation between men and women. Brother Peace announces itself as 'men breaking silence to end men's violence' and calls 'on all men to help stop the war against women'. The poster defines the basis of trust and cooperation by suggesting actions that connect social responsibility and social justice to masculinity and male power in our society. It does this for both the public and private spheres of men's and women's lives and in so doing calls for a reordering of social conduct.

The kind of theorizing feminists have struggled to develop over the past twenty-five years is finding its place in men's consciousness-raising groups and social activism efforts as well as in the academic community. Some years ago when I was reviewing research for a paper on the social psychology of rape (Cherry 1983) I discovered how little was written about the use of violence in men's lives compared to the growing body of work on women's experience of and resistance to victimization. While feminist research had extended its theoretical framework in ways I have already outlined, relative silence[5] prevailed in our understanding of men's daily lives. Let me again use rape as an example. Kirkpatrick and Kanin's (1957) data in the 1950s revealed a substantial degree of victimization of American college-age women. Following women's reports of sexual coercion with men known to them, Kanin (1969) also studied college-age men who reported an extensive use of coercion in their encounters with women. Several years elapsed before the phenomenon of date-rape was named and studied more extensively in the context of male sexual socialization and behavioural practices (Lottes 1988). In general, the study of men *qua* men has, for a long time, been missing in the analysis of violence towards women except for those few men incarcerated in prisons and mental institutions.

But there has been some movement. In 1975, the same year as Susan Brownmiller's publication of *Against Our Will: Men, Women and Rape*, an entire issue of the *Journal of Social Issues*, a periodical consistently devoted to social problems and social change, was concerned with the Vietnam war. Brownmiller analysed the extensiveness of rape in wartime, using the Vietnam War and the My Lai massacre of 16 March 1968 as one of the most horrific examples of wartime rape. While there was no direct discussion of wartime rape in the *Journal of Social Issues*, Eisenhart (1975) did acknowledge the link between masculinity, sexuality, and aggressivity:

> The sexuality of Vietnam veterans was systematically assaulted and shaped in training ... a frustrated sexuality became linked with violence and aggression. One young veteran I have worked with became completely impotent three years after discharge. Unable to maintain an erection during the last three attempts at intercourse, he was afraid to try again. At this time he purchased a weapon, a pistol, and began brandishing and discharging it. His sexuality was blocked by a frustrated idealized male role which could not tolerate intimacy. The means to affirm manhood was through face-to-face combat, aggressive behavior, and the seeking of dominance.
>
> (Eisenhart 1975: 21–2)

Eisenhart did not spell out the implications of combat training for such an individual's subsequent treatment of women. He wrote of the work he was doing with Vietnam veterans, and stated that 'many Vietnam veterans that I have worked with report sexual frustration, a fear of intimacy, and strong urges to "kill somebody".' While Eisenhart did not pursue the implications in his article, in Brownmiller's writings we find evidence that women have been the legitimate targets for sexual assault in wartime and after.

The question of rape was omitted from the social psychological study of the Vietnam war and at a later date it was still only peripherally important to a social psychological examination of the male sex role. In an issue of the *Journal of Social Issues* devoted to the male experience, only one article by Alan Gross (1978) touched on violence towards women. There were no articles discussing issues of date-rape, wife-battering, incest or sexual harassment as part of male experience. This is not surprising given that many of these phenomena were still in the process of being named by feminist researchers and explored predominantly from the vantage point of the female victims and/or survivors. However, by 1981, an entire issue of the *Journal of Social Issues* was devoted to the study of rape and while still focused primarily on the female victims of rape, one article by Neil Malamuth reviewed research to date bearing on how men assessed the likelihood that they would use rape under various conditions. For example, he asked men in a variety of studies to 'indicate their responses on a five point scale ranging from (1) not at all likely to (5) very likely', 'that they personally would rape if they could be assured of not being caught and punished' (Malamuth 1981: 140). I read this article with great interest in part because it built on earlier indications in the 1950s and 1960s that a relatively large percentage of men (20 per cent averaged across many studies scored above the mid-point on the question asked) would resort to coercion. It was clear that the phenomenon had not ceased, only the study of it.

It seems increasingly possible that our understanding of the particulars of everyday male experience with sexual coercion might now become part of the study of men's lives and the construction of masculinity from a male perspective. Malamuth has contributed by defining some of the parameters of 'rape proclivity' and linked it to nonsexual forms of aggression and men's interest in pornography. This might serve as a model for examining other types of violence towards women which have been conceptually linked by feminist analysis. How do men learn and use various forms of coercion and violence? Could we learn as much from qualitative work in this field as we have from qualitative work on female victimization? Coercive sexuality undoubtedly takes different forms in different men's lives and narrative techniques might provide a better sense of the particulars of men's lives. Moving away from the laboratory to study women's experience with victimization has shown us that we can accumulate an understanding well beyond laboratory findings.

Malamuth located 'rape proclivity' as an aspect of social learning theory and the processes of behavioural inhibition and disinhibition. Feminist theorizing and research suggest that rape proclivity is better located in the dual frameworks of gender roles and power/dominance relations. The latter perspective takes into account learned sex-roles but it goes further and requires an examination of how gender socialization combines with power – economic, legal and political – to affect the lives of men and women. Rape proclivity means something at both a psychological and societal level. A man who indicates that he is rape-prone is saying something about himself and how he might behave as well as something about his society and its tolerance of both the abuse of power and the abuse of women as legitimate targets.

There remains a relative silence about rape, wife-battering, incest, sexual harassment and sex discrimination from a male perspective. There are, however, the beginnings of a psychology of men and men's studies (for example, Brod 1987) in which a well-articulated account of violence in men's lives becomes possible. I think it is particularly pressing to examine the lives of men who have resisted the use of violent and coercive strategies and to examine the lives of men engaged alongside women in the struggle to end violence. How much do we know about how men arrived at these life choices? How much do we know about men who themselves have been victimized by sexual and physical assault?

When I began university teaching in 1974, many male undergraduates were interested in studying the problems of women, their fears of success and other afflictions. In the past few years, I have been encouraged that several men have shown more interest in studying male experience. They have wanted to study the men who batter their wives, the exploitation of black male sexuality in white pornography, the experience of expectant fathers, men's responses to feminism and more. The men who want to study what is wrong with women seem to have beaten a retreat, at least from my door. I taught my course on 'Social Problems' twice during the 1980s as 'The Male Gender Role' with an open and good natured response from the men who took the course either by mistake or expecting it to cover a range of social issues. I am not so certain this would be the response with the chillier campus climate of the 1990s.

However, as we read articles by and about men, theorizing about male violence towards women will change. For feminist researchers, the study of women has provided a much needed corrective to the caricatures of women found in the traditional research literature. Feminists have some-times argued that the problems studied and the interpretations made in social psychology suffer from masculine bias when, in fact, much of social psychology is actually about 'subject populations' and 'general laws of social behaviour'. It cannot be automatically assumed that the main-stream literature tells us about men *qua* men any more than about women. Indeed, the masculine bias has been a universalizing and gender-neutralizing bias rather than a particularizing bias in social psychological theory construction.

Social psychological theorizing has developed within the framework of general psychology conceptualized as a predictive physical science. The discipline presents us with a literature about the general behaviour of the 'average person'. When we look further at who theorizes and does research, it is clearer that this universalizing habit is constructed through studies of particular subject groups and research practices that describe a standard of white, male and middle-class values and normative behaviours (Wallston and Grady 1985). Feminist theorists can run into the same difficulties if we try to talk about 'women' in some generic or universal sense. At some point, we need to draw attention more clearly in all research to the limitations of our knowledge representations. We need to ask whose interests are served by the research we do? Who have we included and who have we excluded in our theoretical accounts? What steps have we taken to discuss the limitations of our theoretical framework?

I find myself constantly working between the conceptual poles of over-generalizing and over-particularizing. Just as soon as I have said something about 'women' I find it requires qualification and for this reason theorizing is a very tentative business intended for constant revising and rethinking. What troubles me in contemporary social psychology is that we have moved too far towards the pole of generalization at the expense of meaningful differences among people. The individual personality differences which often interest social psychologists are not the ones that historically figure so prominently in the daily lives of large numbers of people, namely, gender, race, class, age and sexual orientation.

In the study of interpersonal aggression, the experience of women victimized by male violence was at one time clouded by the language of 'subjects', 'independent' and 'dependent' variables. The laboratory methods of acquiring knowledge have sometimes obscured knowledge that women needed to have to survive. Feminist social theories bring words to women's experience so that women can make sense of their lives and the inequities in them. These words can reflect moments of powerful insight mobilizing us for social change. Social psychological theorizing has to be more than an intellectual puzzle for those outside the dominant culture in any way – as female, black, aboriginal, poor or elderly. For those in non-dominant and marginalized groups, theorizing is part of a larger struggle to be heard among ourselves and to change the dominant culture's economic and psychological impact on our lives. As we try to explain acts of violence, we empower ourselves to take action against violence. Feminist theorizing can become a powerful mode of resistance and a spur to reordering personal, social and institutional arrangements.

Chapter 4

Hardening of the categories and other ailments

[I]n the minute world of subatomic particles the presence of an observer and his observing device is likely to alter the swing of things, but we are only beginning to recognize how in a world of sticks and stones and men and bones, point of view not only determines what is seen, but to some extent at least manipulates the very being of it. The field glasses literally affect the bird, as we immediately realize when we notice that the bird's true environment is not that little close-up of branches and twigs that the field glasses disclose but as well the field, the field glasses, and the breathing thing that looks through them. If the man carrying the field glasses carries also a shotgun, the nature of the bird's being is likely abruptly to change. But if that bird watcher does nothing more than take up space and continue breathing, in most subtle ways he changes the bird's world – because he has intruded into it. He is a pressure that was not there and now is. The bird, of course, also changes the man. A rapport is created, a dialogue of interests that cuts across the field and – at least from the man's point of view – modifies the world not only physically but psychologically. And ultimately again physically. A man sees a bird and responds to the sight. His feelings, his arousal, starts a whole progress of synaptic clickings; his blood chemistry modifies ever so slightly; his fingers tighten – and a bit more carbon dioxide is available to the grass, a fraction less oxygen to the bird. Mind is entangled in being and, observing well, observes that fact.

(Unterecker 1973: vii–viii)

I live in Ottawa, Canada's capital city, in a winter climate that ranks second to Ulan Bator, Mongolia's capital, for recorded low temperatures. Field research is a seasonal occupation at best unless you happen to be at my university, Carleton University, which connects buildings by an extensive underground network of tunnels navigated by electric 'golf-carts'. Students who live in campus residences are referred to as tunnel rats because they do not appear outdoors or above ground between November and March. We do not have a specialization in the social psychology of underground living but we probably should have.

Undeterred by climate, I have sent students in my social psychology research seminar out into those tunnels to observe and bring back stories of their fellow humans. I try to teach them that the investigative practices they use are not 'neutral' tools but are themselves part of shaping their observations. To accomplish this I often use a study published in *Science* in 1976 by Jenni and Jenni. This study involves an observational analysis of book-carrying behaviour and its pedagogical utility lies in the remarkable contrast it provides between a seemingly simple behaviour and the realm of theoretical complexity required to interpret it.

The Jennis' study involves their categorization of book-carrying into two main types. They devised a coding scheme that divides the world of carrying books into Type I and Type II methods. Type I behaviour is coded as resting books on the hip or in front of the body, while Type II is coded as pinching the books from above or supporting them from below. Women more typically manifest Type I behaviours while men display Type II. The various possibilities are depicted in Figure 4.1.

In using this study, I first ask my students to go out into the tunnels and look at the world the way the Jennis do and when they come up out of the tunnels they are invariably convinced that the Jennis have distorted reality. They are convinced they have seen more variability out there and they come up with at least two or three additional categories for coding behaviour. This is quite possible; the Jennis do note several kinds of variation, among them age and regional differences. Also, we are, as I've mentioned, a winter location and you might expect that many of us have

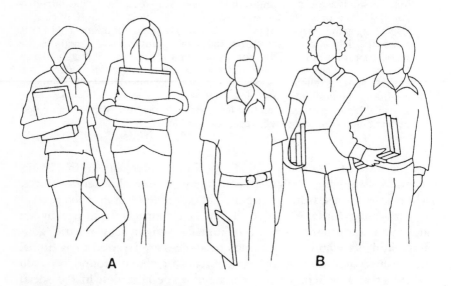

A   B

Figure 4.1 Methods of carrying books
Note: (A) In all Type I carrying methods, the short edges of the books rest on the hip or in front of the body. (B) In Type II methods, the books are either pinched from above or supported from below by the hand or the hand and arm.
Source: Reproduced from Jenni and Jenni 1976: 859

backpacks permanently stitched into our outerwear. We are also a campus that is relatively hospitable to a person with impaired mobility. Modern wheelchairs are decked out with baskets and ledges for book-carrying, Type III carrying behaviour if you will. Then there's those people who carry their briefcases the 'male' way and their books the 'female' way. Is a lap-top computer to be coded as a book? What should be done with those souls who by outward appearance cannot be coded 'male=1' and 'female=2'? Are we going to let these 'differences' ruin a perfectly good study?

Leaving the 'noise' aside, we do manage to replicate the study with respect to its finding of a sex difference. It becomes my job to convince them that generality matters more than individuality, homogeneity more than variability. I rarely do a satisfactory job at this because I enjoy invention, novelty, difference and cultural variation. So, sometimes, to do my job, I have to resort to brute authority. After all, I tell them, I'm the professor and if they expect a grade, they should code two categories and either forget what else they saw or learn to call it error variance. Inter-rater reliability takes on a whole new dimension with this approach. Some of them rebel and complain of my hypocrisy. How can I ask them to observe for themselves and then insist on two categories of book-carrying behaviour?

'But you saw them both with your own eyes', I flash back.

'Not before you told us what to look for', one argues.

'And if I hadn't told you?' I ask.

'Who knows what we might have seen', says one.

There is always one student who wedges his or her voice into the ruckus and wants to know why we're arguing about this anyway. Aren't we all just people and what does it really matter how we carry our books? The voice comes from outside the parameters of the conversation; it could be a parent at the dinner table telling us to stop fighting or a meta-observer who seeks a broader meaning to our debate. Whoever it is, it is a voice that lets us know that we have been observed observing. I take it as my cue to switch to explanation and escape from the clutches of our inability to agree once and for all on what's out there and whether we 'see' in some clear and unambiguous way.

We strike a truce and agree that variability is 'interesting' but that generally a few categories take in most cases of book-carrying behaviour. How is this to be explained? Even more importantly, how are we to explain this earth-shattering sex difference? What follows is often a very personal discussion about how to account for this quite consistent difference between the sexes, a difference that the Jennis' report is at its peak in the adolescent years. The debate can be even more heated than usual because no important social policy, division of labour in the workplace or sense of inferiority or superiority hinges on the different ways in which men and women carry books. Its seeming triviality acts as a projective test for social prejudice and ideological positions.

'Girls carry their books on their hip shelf because that's how they're going to carry their babies', says a woman with a primordial confidence that would do a sociobiologist proud.

'How can you believe that garbage?' asks another woman, angry at her society and the Academy for failing to liberate this young woman.

'Well, actually, it is probably biological and social', says a conciliatory man, not fully aware that the ground he stands on is hotly contested.

'It's more the way girls are socialized', says another fellow.

'Yeah, what do you know about being a teenage girl?' comes the challenge of the experiential.

'I look at girls. They get all embarrassed when they start to develop and their parents tell them to be modest and cover up', he says. 'Besides, I had sisters'.

'Big deal', says the challenger. 'I grew up female. Of course, we cover ourselves. It's so we don't have to put up with guys leering at us all the time. It's a form of social protest'.

Quickly, we have run from biology to politics. I listen to the students debate what they believe and confront each other's positions with little in the way of 'scientific evidence'.

The Jennis' research rarely fails to catalyse a debate about the social significance of infrequent events. It sets off arguments about what is to be included and what is to be excluded in our categorizations of the social world, our methods of gathering evidence (did anyone ever ask a book-carrier why s/he carries books that way?) and our interpretations. We are always scrapping over the particulars and studies like the Jennis' call forth a display of the deep commitments we have to positions that explain the most trivial of social behaviours. Yet, it is precisely because they use a 'particular' instance of our social behaviour that interconnects our physical, sociocultural and political worlds that the research has the capacity to evoke different points of view.

While a discussion of sex differences in book-carrying behaviour can raise the room temperature a few degrees, were I to substitute a discussion of sex differences in achievement or aggressivity, one would virtually see steam on the windows. Martha Mednick (1989) has nicely tackled the politics of many of our well-known psychological constructions for explaining sex differences – fear of success, androgyny, a different voice. I'll use the example of androgyny to go into greater depth on this matter of interpreting differences. Mednick writes:

> The concept of androgyny was advanced in the mid-1970s as the answer to the puzzle of gender; it represented a new look at conceptions about measurement of masculinity and femininity. At that level, it was an

excellent critique. . . . It was the subject of considerable psychological research; at least three new scales were developed to measure it, and it spawned numerous dissertations. It was also widely discussed by feminist scholars in other social science disciplines and in the humanities. . . . Even more than the fear of success, it became a buzz word for the public and was personified in advertising, fashion, cosmetics for men and rock musicians such as Boy George, Michael Jackson and Prince. Although androgyny has not passed from the scene, it has not been very helpful, particularly in its popularized version, in solving the problem of gender.

(Mednick 1989: 1119)

Despite questions concerning its scientific merit, androgyny has retained its popularity. Androgyny was an appealing social critique that for the first time allowed feminist researchers to challenge the non-overlapping categories of masculine and feminine. While its politics have come to be seen as promoting self-contained individualism (Sampson 1977) and the conservative political agenda that focuses on personal rather than social change (Mednick 1989), it is a very useful historical example to work with if we're trying to understand how we categorize and explain the social world. As a construct, it was transitional between the rigidity of conceptualizing men and women as masculine or feminine and more recent notions of socially and politically constructed masculinity and femininity.

It is important to remember that Sandra Bem (1974, 1983), as researcher and parent, was confronting established developmental and personality theorists who maintained that gender-role consistency was equivalent to well-being, mental health and sexual adjustment. Take for example a quote from the *Handbook of Socialization Theory and Research* (Mussen 1969) as representative of prevailing views:

Parents have two major tasks in promoting their child's sex-typing. The first is tuition, i.e. teaching the child appropriate sex-typed responses through rewards and punishments, and guiding his behavior, directing it into the proper channels. The second is providing a model of the proper general attitudes and personality characteristics for the child to emulate. Fortunately, most parents can perform these tasks without great difficulty because they themselves have absorbed and incorporated sex-appropriate responses, characteristics and attitudes and they have clear conceptions of appropriate masculine and feminine behaviors.

(Mussen 1969: 728)

I had spent several years in the early 1970s thinking of ways to subvert sex-typing and to disinhibit adult women and men from avoiding activities considered inappropriate for their gender. It occurred to me that the process might have to take place at an earlier age and that I didn't know much about the process of becoming those sex-typed adults who were walking into my experimental social psychology laboratory. In graduate school I had devoted much time and effort to understanding adult women's achievement behaviour. I wanted to learn more about children's play environments. I began to collaborate with a developmental psychologist, Candace Schau, on a project that took us into the lives of pre-school children at play (Schau et al. 1980). Not unlike book-carrying behaviour, sex differences in play behaviour and toy preferences were seemingly well-established findings in the literature. However, many studies rested their case on forcing children to choose between cars and dolls and did not watch children playing without adult intervention.

In our study, we introduced what we called 'neutral' toys, that is, toys that were not clearly sex-typed. So, in the case of a manipulable toy, a large children's toy manufacturer had several varieties that we selected as masculine (e.g. a drill), feminine (e.g. a food mixer) and neutral (e.g. a movie camera). We had these three modes for a variety of play activities – puppets, building sets, read-along stories and figurine sets (e.g. farm animals, action heroes, etc.).

What I found most interesting in our research was not that children engaged in some degree of sex-typed behaviour with little or no formal pressure to do so. All of this seemed quite compatible with the mass-marketing strategies of toys on television and the sex-segregated shelves of large toy stores. That boys were more strongly sex-typed in their choices than girls was also quite consistent with previous research. What intrigued me was that the system was not perfect. Girls slipped through it at an alarming rate and this offered a subversive sort of hope for later life choices. Not only that, parents' expectations that their children would play with culturally defined sex-appropriate toys were, in general, inaccurate. Mothers were accurate in their predictions of their daughters' play with feminine toys. They were inaccurate regarding their daughters' play with masculine and neutral toys and inaccurate regarding their sons' play with feminine toys. Fathers' predictions were not accurate for either sons or daughters for any toy–gender type.

Children, especially females, were at times remarkably more 'androgynous' than parents and researchers could see. The early work on androgyny throughout the 1970s was somewhat liberating for adult women's sex-typed behaviour – it legitimated assertiveness and achievement while honouring nurturance and expressiveness. It made us as parents and researchers more aware of our own 'androgyny' and it challenged Mussen's earlier dictum that most parents can teach their children sex-typed behaviour because 'they themselves have absorbed and incorporated sex-appropriate responses, characteristics, and attitudes'. While perhaps most parents can teach these roles, many did not want to.

What we see in the world and often give name to is in many ways what we think we should see. Our explanations, scientific or otherwise, guide the categories for coding data. If the researcher is ambivalent about the desirability of men and women taking on the same roles, it is likely that the categorization system will reflect this. Just as theories are neither 'value-free' nor 'neutral', so too our categories for coding the social world often reflect what we would like to see. Particularly when we are studying the world of infants and small children, it has recently been argued that our theories are more a reflection of the inner world of the researcher than the researched (Bradley 1989).

As I started watching children play, I started thinking that 'masculinity', 'femininity' and 'androgyny' were in fact ways of describing humanly constructed environments, not individual facets of persons. Our world of material objects – playtoys, activities, clothing – is constructed along gendered dimensions and inevitably becomes a powerful 'teacher' of young children. That world of objects is mediated by adults who can choose to deny dolls and pink shirts to boys, doctor's kits and trains to girls. I spent many hours watching children play with other children and with their parents and many more hours looking at the way pre-schools were designed to include and exclude one sex or the other in a particular activity.

In reviewing the literature on sex-typing, I came across a study in the developmental psychology literature by Lynn and De Palma Cross (1974), entitled 'Parent preference of preschool children'. It was assumed in this study that the process of sex-role socialization is dependent on identification with the same-sex parent. This identification follows upon a recognition by the child of him/herself as male or female (in cognitive-developmental terms) or a recognition by the child of him/herself as the same or different from the initial caretaker, usually the mother (in identification theory terms). In the case of social learning theory, the similarity between parent as model and child as observer is a mechanism for learning a particular sex role. The study was based on pre-school children in the late 1960s and was consistent with the ideology expressed in the passage quoted from the *Handbook of Socialization Theory and Research* (see above, p. 45).

I requested the raw data for this study from Lynn and De Palma Cross[1] because I had some new questions I thought I might be able to find answered. While the mechanism suggested for learning sex-typed behaviour has been chiefly same-sex parent identification, there is no overwhelming empirical evidence in support of this. Maccoby and Jacklin (1974) raised considerable doubt about the process of parent identification as the primary mechanism for sex-role socialization, given the wide variety of sources from which children can draw information. From my vantage point as a single parent, I too found it an oversimplification of the way my own child seemed to be making use of the men and women available to him. On the other hand, the article by Lynn and De Palma Cross (1974) seemed to support same-sex parent identification. These authors stated the matter of sex-role learning as follows:

> Very young boys, perceiving that they belong to a different sex category from the mother, are strongly motivated to avoid being feminine and to acquire masculine characteristics. This should be reflected in an overall tendency to prefer being with the father as a model of masculinity. At first, this preference for being with the father rather than the mother should be particularly strong, because, still being insecure in their sex role, boys would be particularly anxious not to remain identified with the mother. Thus, being in fact poorly identified with masculinity, he should strongly reject the mother and prefer being with the father. Girls, in contrast, being generally of the same sex as their initial caretaker (usually the mother), and requiring no sex-role shift, should experience no powerful motivation to be with the parent of the same sex.

> (Lynn and De Palma Cross 1974: 556)

In fact, these authors reported that boys and girls, by age 4, chose same-sex parents as partners in their play activities to a greater extent than opposite-sex parents. I thought it worthwhile to look more closely at the findings of Lynn and De Palma Cross. While they had gathered their data in the late 1960s, my observations of pre-school children a decade later suggested far more variability. I was also influenced by the adult preferences of my own son that seemed largely based on availability and not gender in our cooperative living arrangement.

In the study by Lynn and De Palma Cross, children were provided with seven opportunities to choose either their mother or father as a play partner. The toys and activities chosen by the investigators were 'neutral' toys, e.g. Etch-a-sketch, blocks, stick-on-animals. They 'seemed not to be stereotyped for a parent of a given sex' (Lynn and De Palma Cross 1974: 557). It occurred to us that androgynous parent preference, that is, the choice of one parent being as good as another, would be maximal with a neutral toy where the expectations are that either parent could be expected to know how to play and where the child would be making socially desirable responses either way.

In Lynn and De Palma Cross's study, children's choices were tabulated and if four or more choices out of seven were for the mother, the child was categorized as mother-preferring, and conversely for categorization as father-preferring. At age 4, these authors reported a significant chi-square, indicating that boys preferred fathers and girls preferred mothers as play partners ($\chi^2 = 5.6$, df = 1, p 0.05).

My first interest was in re-analysing the data according to a different construction of parent preference. A large number of children were choosing mother or father three or four times out of seven. These children, to my way of categorizing them, were more equal-preferring than strongly same- or opposite-sex preferring. Let's examine the data more carefully for four-year-olds as an example. According to Lynn and De Palma Cross's breakdown, the twenty-nine four-year olds they studied appear same-sex preferring (see Table 4.1).

Table 4.1 Four-year-olds' preferences for mother or father

	Proportion mother-preferring	Proportion father-preferring
Boys	0.41 (n = 12)	0.59 (n = 17)
Girls	0.72 (n = 21)	0.28 (n = 8)
	(χ^2 = 5.6, df = 1, p < 0.05)	

Source: Adapted from Lynn and De Palma Cross, Table 1, Frequency distribution of mother –father preference by age and sex (1974)

However, if a three-way analysis is performed using the same children but dividing them into those who are mother- or father-preferring (5, 6 or 7 choices of that parent) and those who are equal-preferring (3 or 4 choices of that parent), the chi-square is no longer significant (χ^2 = 3.68, df = 2, n.s.) and a larger percentage of the children appears equal-preferring than one-parent preferring (see Table 4.2).

Table 4.2 Re-analysis of four-year-olds' preferences for mother or father or both

	Proportion preferring:		
	Mother	Equal	Father
Boys	0.24	0.41	0.34
Girls	0.38	0.48	0.14
	(χ^2 = 3.68, df = 2, n.s.)		

Fully 41 per cent of boys and 48 per cent of girls at age 4 were equal-preferring, an increase from ages 2 and 3. One could argue that by age 4, some of these boys and girls were beginning to increase their utilization of both parents in games and activities. This study was not a thorough longitudinal investigation of the actual balance struck by these parents as caretakers and active play partners, but it at least suggested, when re-analysed, that in an environment that provides gender neutral toys and activities, children have the capacity to interact with both parents and learn from each.

If children make their preferences of parents as play partners, taking into account the parent's gender and his or her expectations for sex-appropriate play, then the re-analysis of Lynn and De Palma Cross's data seems quite reasonable. If the toy is neutral, either parent will do, as was the case when the analysis was constructed according to a different criterion of mother and/or father preference.

One might further expect that mothers would be more often chosen for play if the toy is feminine sex-typed; fathers, if the toy is masculine sex-typed (Duncan 1980). A choice measure cannot tell us whether the child acts as s/he does out of competence (i.e. sex-role knowledge) or a motive to appear socially desirable by meeting parent expectations for sex-appropriate behavioural choices. However, such a pattern would show just how early young children can reproduce the gender-linked behaviours appropriate to given situations and how situationally dependent and easily modifiable their behaviour can be.

The sex-typing of toys in our society and the power of parents in eliciting appropriate behavioural choices cannot be underestimated. However, neutral toys in environments where adult pressures are absent may also show us another side of children – their capacity for both assertive and nurturant play. With respect to activities and tasks, there may also be greater variability than some might find in academic research. A few years after my research in preschools ended, I happened to be visiting a preschool in my neighbourhood while parents were arriving with their children. Once the parents had left and the day had begun, several of the children were eager to play dress-up, and I was treated to a splendid drag show, a regular event, according to the staff. How many parents would have called an emergency meeting if they had seen their sons and daughters cross-dressing and cross-behaving is difficult to estimate. Even more interesting is whether the children would have interrupted their activities if their parents had suddenly appeared on the scene. At 4, the gender role variability is still reasonably acceptable. At 7 and 8 there is more concern expressed and certainly our adult labour force continues to reflect an ambivalence about changing our beliefs that boys can do what girls do and vice-versa. What is of interest to me as a researcher and social psychologist is the complicated interplay among our beliefs as parents, researchers and activists in the way we shape, categorize and 'see' what is there to be seen.

Chapter 5

Self-investigating consciousness from different points of view

so where am I now that I see
that art is science
the tinkering, the manipulating,
the conscious carpentry and construction
the what if
and that science is art, the emotional, the passionate,
the truly irrational sense of discovery from nothing
to something new
and now that everything is stood on its end
like I was when I was born
and could hear only my mother's voice
with no worldly language to make out her meaning
where am I now that I see
everything upside down again?
(Author's Journal, 22 November 1986)

I have always had an intense curiosity about what makes us who we are. I was drawn to psychology for this reason and was enthralled by my introductory psychology professor's speculations on the reticular activating system and its role in consciousness. I spent long hours reflecting on how I, myself, was thinking with my mind about my brain . . . or was it with my brain about my mind . . . and who was 'I' anyway? Was there a specific location for consciousness?

Those questions led me to a philosophy of mind class in which the professor assigned a book, *Human Senses and Perception* (Wyburn *et al.* 1964) that took different perspectives on the subject of 'mind' – physiological, psychological and philosophical. Within a short span of time, I found a job washing dishes in a neurophysiology lab. I wanted to look inside the head where I was sure I would find the stuff of consciousness and for a time I was content to look for an understanding of human minds inside rats' brains. At that time, it never occurred to me to think of memory, learning and perception as events that arise out of the process of social interaction; for me, these were events that seemed squarely located in the head and quite removed from issues of social justice and social change which also preoccupied me. It also never occurred to me to look for understanding inside my own head as one might in psycho-analysis. In short, as an eighteen-year-old undergraduate my views reflected the received view of psychology common in North American psychology departments of the 1960s, namely, that mind was reducible to brain or behaviour, that mentation and social action were separate spheres and that one's own mind was useful for the study of other minds but not for the study of itself.

I might never have altered my understanding of consciousness from cognitive or neurophysiological functioning to social self-awareness had my own social and political identity not been challenged by the civil rights and women's movements of the 1960s and 1970s. Indeed, it is the impact of these movements that set me on a complicated and non-linear journey into the realm of social psychology, feminist and minority perspectives in psychology, community and social activism, fiction-writing, the study of body/mind awareness techniques and psychoanalysis that resulted in consciousness as the experience of myself – body/mind/spirit – as both separate and inseparable from the social world. That journey has produced a different type of social psychological enquiry.

Researchers have been cautious about using linear models of consciousness-raising that suggest we move from positions of false consciousness as women to a truer consciousness and about using models of social identity that reify an achieved static end point such as a once-and-for-all feminist position. For example, Christine Griffin cautions against using the idea of 'progress' towards a universal way of under-standing feminist consciousness:

> There is no clear distinction between feminist and non-feminists that can operate out of social context, based solely on the personal characteristics or idiosyncratic attitude constellations of individual women.
>
> (Griffin, C. 1989: 188)

Griffin goes on to delineate the many 'pressures which operate to discourage overt feminist allegiance' (Griffin, C. 1989: 191). Ironically, it is these discouraging 'pressures' that might well be the key to understanding similarities in feminist transformation. Studying women's lives through historical documents as well as through the retrospective accounts of contemporary and emerging feminists builds an understanding of the common elements in the process of transformation. Out of the 'stubborn particulars' of women's experiences (alone and together with other women and men) grows an understanding of 'feminist allegiance' through time, culture, race and social class. If social psychological practice has taken a narrative direction, it is out of this need to let the particularities of experience guide the generalities of theorizing. Each of us who has become a feminist has a story to tell that forms part of the transformation of personal and psychological knowledge.[1]

I left my undergraduate studies in psychology in 1969 more or less accepting the idea that the self was best understood through the analysis of personality variables in interaction with social situations. In graduate school I was able to pursue this perspective and incorporate issues of gender into it. I found it easy enough to incorporate the feminist critique of a 'split of human personality' into masculinity–femininity (Constantinople 1973) by working with alternative theories of androgyny (Bem 1974) and sex-role transcendence (Rebecca *et al.* 1976). More difficult to contend with were the critiques of psychology as a discipline that constructed an understanding of womanhood (and women's brains/ minds/consciousness) as biologically and psychologically inferior (Bem and Bem 1970; Parlee 1979; Sheilds 1975; Weisstein 1971). These critiques raised questions about power relations in the discipline itself, in its knowledge-generating and disseminating practices that I began to see in the dyadic relationships of my daily life (e.g. experimenters and subjects; authors and readers; advisors and students; senior faculty and junior faculty). For me, it was the personal experience in power relations both in and out of psychology that transformed the study of 'personality' into the study of 'persons' with political, social, cultural, and gendered identities and it is this transformation that is coincidental with my becoming a feminist and critical psychologist.

When I left graduate school in 1974, my feminist consciousness had yet to become fully integrated with parts of an earlier teenage self that reflected a finely honed sense of social injustice and a commitment to social action. In fact, when I accepted a job as an assistant professor my main sentiments were relief and excitement at the prospect of finally earning a salary. I spent very little time thinking about what it would be like as the only woman in an all-male working environment. At 21, I had worked as one of the first women integrating an all-male mental health facility and I frankly thought it could be no worse than that. I saw the whole business as an adventure, packed all my belongings in my car and headed off to dazzle the world with my factorial designs.

I walked into my new job naively apolitical and ahistorical about women's place in the Academy. I had enjoyed tremendous support as an undergraduate student and felt esteemed by professors who taught me in graduate school. Gender had not seemed to matter personally except in so far as it accounted for a percentage of the variance in my statistical analyses. Within about six months of arriving at my new job, this situation was radically altered. The changes came from personal experiences that challenged my sense of fairness, self-confidence and of legitimately belonging in the Academy. A few examples are in order.

Shortly after I arrived, I was denied faculty housing. While the housing bureau had rented to single male faculty, it was not willing to rent to single female faculty. I fought this discriminatory policy, won my case and had the policy changed but not without being subjected to a level of verbal abuse that seems to flow naturally from those desperate to maintain the *status quo*. Not too long after this, a senior member of a departmental committee reviewing my progress came to speak to me about the concerns he had that my research on gender was becoming too applied for the Psychology Department. Although they had hired me to work in the area of gender, he wanted me to realize that the non-experimental path on which I was embarking would not be favourably received. But not to worry, he would protect me by explaining my work to the review committee. Of course, I felt extremely vulnerable with my fate in the hands of a senior colleague who was known for creating anxiety among junior faculty.

For the three years before leaving to return to Canada in 1977, there were almost daily reminders that I was a gendered being. I remember, soon after my arrival, a woman who passed by my office door, back-tracked and yelped, 'I don't believe it, they've hired a woman!' I remember a less than tactful colleague standing at my door hemming and hawing until finally he came out with, 'My wife says that most female professors who stay single are lesbians.' I remember the days before sexual harassment policies when I would arrive at work to find sexually explicit notes under my door from a colleague in a position to judge my work and the feelings of helplessness, disillusionment and self-blame that would ensue. As many of us were to find out with the research of the 1980s, none of these experiences was unusual for women in any segment of the labour force.

On the one hand, these first experiences as an academic created feelings of isolation and self-doubt and sometimes an inability to develop as a responsible educator, researcher and colleague. On the other hand, they started to politicize my life and my work and to connect me to those with similar experiences. I began to read the history of psychology and its often exclusionary and damaging practices of studying women, racial and ethnic minorities. I became involved in the newly developing women's studies programme; in the minority recruitment programmes on campus; in developing a social psychology field placement for black students in the local affirmative action office and many other activities. My allies were those as interested as I was in seeing the university become more inclusive in its student and faculty composition, in what it teaches and takes to be important. In many ways, my actions were beginning to connect with the kinds of social action projects that engaged me in my teens and early twenties. However, my consciousness about social change was changing.

Within about one year of arriving at my first academic job, my personal and intellectual worlds were no longer made up of 'personalities' and 'individual differences' and my practice of social psychology had little choice but to change. I had responded to the categorization of me as a certain kind of woman – a feminist – with an emotional awareness of the social and political implications of the label. I found myself attending to my students' social identities – their sex, race, social class, age, sexual orientation – and wanting to hear their stories. In my own mind, I worked with a kind of calculus I now think of as the PQ (Privilege Quotient). It occurred to me that one could predict incomes and outcomes not by knowing a person's score on a balanced authoritarianism scale but by knowing where the person stood in the PQ hierarchy that seemed so overdetermining in shaping a life course.

In all of this, there was one incident that stands out among others as a kind of turning point of feminist consciousness and allegiance – a bridge crossed that engaged my energies at a deeper level of political commitment and that angered me beyond measure. It happened quite casually, at a faculty meeting at which I was the only woman present. We were in the process of hiring a new faculty member. A woman who had been shortlisted for the position would have been interviewed had a colleague not pointed out that she was having an affair with a professor in another part of the country and would probably not accept the position. I protested, pointing out that her personal situation had nothing to do with her professional aspirations and that our efforts to recruit her should continue. I heard my voice among the 'other' voices in a very new way, namely, as a member of the group called 'women' for whose rights I felt compelled to fight. That small gesture of resistance was to become a very significant psychological turning point.

Despite many other examples of injustice, I remember this incident as one of the most transformative. Up to that point – 1975 – I had not relinquished my belief that universities could be set apart from the 'real' world. I believed the university could be a refuge where discrimination and harassment would only occasionally enter and where merit and competence were more generally the rule. Over time, those scoring low on the PQ scale would make their way into the academic ranks through their competence and the assumed benevolence of the Academy. What I saw in this incident symbolized all the poor excuses given for the arrogant history of excluding women, blacks and gays (among others) from the Academy and from the production and dissemination of academic knowledge; it had happened to so many women regardless of merit and it could have happened to me. It was then I understood how much more than benign neglect it would take to change universities. The Academy was not benign; it was much like other institutions with little social accountability – a place of privilege in our society and a turf protected by those who inherit its rewards.

I remember that this incident moved me to consider my own privilege. How had I come as far as I had educationally? What cracks had I slipped through and how? The answer lies in a mixture of personal and societal circumstances that form the unique way in which my temperament and abilities intersected with the PQ that set both limits and opportunities for me relative to others. Some factors were obvious. For example, it helped that the economy in Canada in the mid-1960s offered readily available summer work, that universities were expanding, and that the Ontario government had a decent system of tuition fees, student loans and awards, not to mention good support for graduate work in the early 1970s. This was also a time when the doors to professional and graduate schools were opening for white women like myself. These organizational and systemic benefits helped because, while my almost middle-class Jewish family had stressed education as a means of advancement throughout my life, I never saw them as financially secure enough to be able to assist me very much.

What is more difficult to describe are those murky levels of attachment that play themselves out in life-long idiosyncratic patterns. For this I find fiction-writing a more suitable medium for expression. Perhaps I can offer this as a way of understanding my sense of belonging in the Academy and my tenacity in the face of challenges to my legitimacy as a woman. As a young girl, I used to play 'school' and I would play the teacher in front of an imaginary class. I had a special affection for the paraphernalia of the job – books, notepads, coloured pencils, yellow chalk. It never seemed to bother my parents that I stole chalk from school or talked out loud to imaginary students as long as I wiped the chalk marks off our small apartment walls. So for me, becoming an academic allowed me to continue to play in my parents' approving presence.

In later years when the playing got rough, it helped to engage in a bit of denial and more make-believe. Once on a return trip home from graduate school, I asked an old friend what had happened to all the women in our undergraduate philosophy club. He regretfully informed me that there were no other women. I suppose I had conjured them up to feel less odd for belonging to an all-male club at the age of 18. And there I was at 28, once again the only woman in an all-male club but this time unable to deny or pretend that the absence of women was somehow just an accident, lack of qualifications or of their own free choice.

You might like to know that we did not interview the female candidate for the job but instead interviewed and hired the next person on the list – a quite competent man. I must also tell you that I was not the only one to feel the injustice of these events. A male colleague who supported my objections in the meeting at which I spoke out found himself increasingly the object of his colleagues' concerns. I learned from his experience how difficult it was for men in those days, though perhaps less so now, to ally with feminists and still retain the respect and approval of men if they wanted that. Each of us has some points in the privilege game – skin colour, class, friends in high places – and if we don't play the game by the rules in place, we may be in for a very rough time of it, female and male.

Through all these experiences, prejudice and discrimination were the 'objects' of my study in social psychology. Once they became part of my subjective experience and once I shared experiences with other marginalized people, the distinction between subject and object was increasingly difficult to maintain. Ultimately, it transformed the kind of social psychology I have come to practise and teach – one that values narrative as well as experimental techniques for examining power relations and social identities. The liberation movements of the 1960s and 1970s created for many women a practice of consciousness-raising and self-analysis that ultimately has transformed the kind of non-reflexive social science we were taught to do.

While most of the 'raw data' for my understanding came from my immediate experiences and talking with other women and minorities, I also started collecting other people's written stories of transformation. In the early 1970s I collected manifestos of various minority groups, primarily in the United States where I was living at the time. For me, they illustrate that models of feminist and minority awareness and allegiance are best understood in historical context. The manifestos I collected represent the writings of numerous groups.[2] They express that phase where the Privilege Quotient is challenged collectively and individually, where a sense of injustice has been ignited and consciousness is transformed, where conscious and non-conscious collaboration with one's victimization is changed to resistance. The language of these documents of the early 1970s seems quite exaggerated to me now, paradoxically inclusionary and exclusionary. I find myself amused by the tone of self-righteousness and taken aback by the unabashed anger for 'the Other'. Yet, it was these manifestos that captured something of my own process of consciousness-raising and its impact on how I have come to practise social psychology.

Let me describe three of them: 'The Fourth World manifesto' by Barbara Burris[3] (Burris 1971) (in agreement with K. Barry, T. Moore, J. DeLor, J. Parent, C. Stadelman); 'A personal manifesto' from *Chicano Manifesto* by Armando Rendon (Rendon 1971) and 'Refugees from Amerika: A gay manifesto' by Carl Wittman (Wittman 1972). Each manifesto is a statement of personal and political change, of defining the oppression of the group with which the person identifies, of separating him or her into self and other, and of expressing the anger that accompanies this sense of

'I' and 'we' versus 'them'. These manifestos were examples to me of the merging of personal experience with political and social advocacy.

THE FOURTH WORLD MANIFESTO

This document was first published in 1971 and came from a desire of some women to take a separate stance from the male-dominated Left and what they saw as the cooptation of anti-imperialist and anti-war women. The theme of women separating from the Left was not limited to the United States in the 1970s (see, for example, Segal 1987). The words are angry and accusatory. The analysis sets female culture apart from 'national' culture that is taken to be the dominant male culture. 'The female culture is the Fourth World' (Burris *et al.* 1971: 355). These women accused the Male Left of being in a 'vicious circle of guilt and righteous-ness' and of being so hung-up on 'who's most oppressed, that they have lost an elemental sense of justice for *all* human beings' (Burris *et al.* 1971: 333, emphasis in original). It would not be easy in the current climate to find a homogenous categorization of 'female culture' that is even over-stated for the time. However, here is what the Fourth World manifesto had to say:

> We find it self-evident that women are a colonized group who have never – anywhere – been allowed self-determination.
>
> (Burris *et al.* 1971: 322)

> We do feel that it is crucial to open up a discussion of the emotional and ideological reasons underlying attempts to co-opt the women's movement into other 'more important' struggles.
>
> (Burris *et al.* 1971: 323)

> We have worked out a deeper analysis of the emotional, psychological, and social assumptions underlying the attitude that women's liberation is less important than black liberation, anti-imperialism, anti-capitalism . . . we criticize the male definition of oppression which does not recognize the unique position of females as a subjugated group.
>
> (Burris *et al.* 1971: 323–4)

> Many women do identify with white and class privileges. Our task as women is not, as the male Left does, to write them off as white bourgeois but to patiently discuss and communicate with women, as sisters, what our true caste position in society is. Once we really under-stand our suppressed caste status and begin to move to free ourselves from it, we women can then understand other groups' oppression – but not before. So the understanding of the oppression of other groups needs to be a very conscious and important part of the Women's Liberation Movement, but only from the basis of an understanding

and struggle for our own freedom as females – not as an imposed lecture by some 'movement organizers' who will 'raise our consciousness' about oppression, and try to impose their white male guilt on us.

(Burris *et al.* 1971: 332)

It is true that women have no recourse other than to rise up in a strong feminist movement to end male domination. We must have our own independent women's movement free from male interference and domination. But we should not lose sight of our ultimate goals. There is a danger that the women's movement will help destroy its own ends if the split between the female and male is made into a new feminist orthodoxy. The women's movement has to be free enough to explore and change the entire range of human relationships and it must be open enough to heal the split between the female and male and draw out the total human potential of every person. If we want to be free as female human beings, we must really be willing to end the split of the human personality that has cut men off from a part of themselves and which has caused untold suffering.

(Burris *et al.* 1971: 357)

This earlier document expressed a breaking off of 'female culture' and a call for solidarity among women that needs to be read against contemporary calls for a greater recognition of diversity among women. I find myself cautious yet stubbornly optimistic about feminist allegiance in light of the events of the intervening twenty-five years – the declining power of the male Left yet the rise of men's movement and men's studies; increased anti-feminism alongside the increasing inclusion of feminists and feminist research at the universities; critiques of the exclusionary aspects of white middle-class feminism and the publication of non-white women's writings; the rise of the right wing agenda that claims to be silenced by the 'political correctness' of new voices in the Academy alongside the growing power of these new voices.

A PERSONAL MANIFESTO

Rendon's manifesto was published in 1971 as a personal statement in the context of a broader political awakening of his Chicano people. Upon college graduation, the author chose a job as a reporter and feature writer for a Catholic weekly newspaper in Sacramento. The editor of the paper gave him permission to cover a 'phenomenon called Cursillos de Cristiandad (Little Courses in Christianity), intense, three day group-sensitivity sessions whose chief objective is the re-Christianization of Catholics' (Rendon 1971: 323). The effect was to challenge his religious beliefs and to radicalize him as a Mexican American. He wrote:

I am a Chicano. What that means to me may be entirely different from
what meaning the word has for you. To be Chicano is to find out something about one's self which has lain dormant, subverted, and nearly
destroyed.

I am a Chicano because of a unique fusion of bloods and history and
culture. I am a Chicano because I sense a rising awareness among
others like myself of a fresh rebirth of self and self-in-others . . .

I am a Chicano in spite of scorn or derision, in spite of opposition
even from my own people, many of whom do not understand and
may never fathom what Chicano means.

(Rendon 1971: 319)

We who call ourselves Chicanos recognize in that word something that
is ours, a name that we have given to ourselves, not one that has been
forced upon us by the Anglo.

. . . I nearly fell victim to the Anglo. My childhood was spent in the
West Side barrio of San Antonio . . . I lived in my grandmother's house
. . . I did well in the elementary grades and learned English quickly.

Spanish was off-limits in school anyway, and teachers and relatives
taught me early that my mother tongue would be of no help in making
good grades and becoming a success. Yet Spanish was the language
I used in playing and arguing with friends. Spanish was the language
I spoke with my *abuelita*, my dear grandmother.

(Rendon 1971: 320–1)

When at the age of ten I went with my mother to California, to the San
Francisco Bay Area where she found work during the war years, I had
my first real opportunity to strip myself completely of my heritage
. . . By the time I graduated from high school and prepared to enter
college, the break was nearly complete.

(Rendon 1971: 321–2)

My ancestry had become a shadow, fainter and fainter about me. I felt
no particular allegiance to it, drew no inspiration from it, and elected
generally to let it fade away. I clicked with the Anglo mind-set in
college, mastered it, you might say. . . . The point of my 'success', of
course, was that I had been assimilated . . .

(Rendon 1971: 322)

My wife and I moved to Sacramento in the fall of 1961 and in a few
weeks the radicalization of this Chicano began. It wasn't a book I read
or a great leader awakening me, for we had no Chavezes or Tijerinas
or Gonzaleses at the time; and it was no revelation from above. It was
my own people who rescued me. There is a large Chicano population
in Sacramento, today one of the most activist in northern California,
but at the time factionalized and still dependent on the social and

church organizations for identity. But together we found each other
... I found my people striving to survive in an alien environment
among foreign people ...

(Rendon 1971: 322–3)

I owe my life to my Chicano people. They rescued me from the Anglo
kiss of death, the monolingual, monocultural, and colorless gringo
society ... Chicano is indefinable, more a word to be understood and
felt and lived than placed in a dictionary or analyzed by Anglo anthro-
pologists, sociologists, and apologists ... It portrays the fact that we
have come to psychological terms with circumstances which might
otherwise cause emotional and social breakdowns among our people
if we only straddle cultures and do not absorb them.

(Rendon 1971: 324–5)

Rendon's awareness of himself as Chicano (and Anglo as 'other') came
from immersion in the group, his language and heritage and his awareness as a man. Through the Cursillo, he 'became reimmersed in a tough,
macho ambiente (an entirely Mexican male environment)' (Rendon 1971:
323). Awareness for Burris and other feminists of her time came from
immersion in 'female culture' and separation from the 'male Left other'.
More than any of the other manifestos from the early 1970s that I
collected, Rendon's was the most personally articulate example of what
that feeling was like to find the core of oneself through shared social
experience. Yet it does not address how we are to balance the exhilara-
tion of finding ourselves as 'woman' or as 'Chicano' with the feelings of
alienation from others defined as 'man' or 'Anglo' or 'Chicana'. Take for
example the recent essay by Angie Chabram-Dernersesian (1992) in
which Rendon's work is subjected to the criticism of male exclusivity
through feminist Chicana analysis. These manifestos are constant
reminders to me of the multiple identities and consciousnesses that form
out of social and political movements for change and how possible it is
to be included and excluded at the same time.

REFUGEES FROM AMERIKA: A GAY MANIFESTO

The issue of multiple identities is further explored in this manifesto,
published in the *San Francisco Free Press*. It began:

San Francisco is a refugee camp for homosexuals. We have fled here
from every part of the nation, and like refugees elsewhere, we came
not because it is so great here, but because it was so bad there. By the
tens of thousands, we fled small towns where to be ourselves would
endanger our jobs and any hope of a decent life; we have fled from
blackmailing cops, from families who disowned or 'tolerated' us; we

have been drummed out of the armed services, thrown out of schools, fired from jobs, beaten by punks and policemen.

And we have formed a ghetto, out of self-protection. It is a ghetto, rather than a free territory, because it is still theirs.

(Wittman 1972: 157)

It should also be clear that these ideas reflect the perspective of one person, and are determined not only by my homosexuality, but my being white, male and middle class. It is my individual consciousness. Our group consciousness will evolve as we get ourselves together – we are only at the beginning.

(Wittman 1972: 158)

On the subject of lesbianism, he wrote:

It's been a male dominated society for too long, and that has warped both men and women. So gay women are going to see things differently from gay men; they are going to feel oppression as women, too. Their liberation is tied up with both gay liberation and women's liberation.

(Wittman 1972: 159)

On the oppression of gays in relation to others and on the idea of a co-alition with other minority groups:

It is important to catalog and understand the different facets of our oppression. There is no future in arguing about degrees of oppression. A lot of 'movement' types come on with a line of shit about homosexuals not being oppressed as much as blacks or Vietnamese or workers or women. We don't happen to fit into their ideas of class (or caste). Bull – when people feel oppressed, they act on that feeling. And we feel oppressed. Talk about the priority of black liberation or ending imperialism over our 'problem' is just antigay propaganda.

(Wittman 1972: 163)

. . . we can't change Amerika alone, we need coalition with other oppressed groups at some point . . . many of us have 'mixed' identities – we are gay, and also we are part of another group trying to free itself – women, blacks, other minority groups . . .

(Wittman 1972: 168–9)

And on Chicanos, he had this to say about their interactions with the gay community:

Basically the same problem as with blacks: trying to overcome mutual animosity and fear, and finding ways to support their movement. The extra problem of superuptightness and machismo among Latin cultures, and the traditional pattern of Mexican 'punks' beating on homosexuals, can be overcome; we're both oppressed, and by the same people at the top. . . . [w]e know the system we're living under is the direct source of oppression, and it's not just a question of sharing the pie. The pie is rotten.

(Wittman 1972: 169)

Whether one accepts that the pie is rotten or not, the pie has been increasingly subdivided over the past twenty-five years to the point where only crumbs are available to society's poorest – often the elderly and women from racial and ethnic minorities. As we move outside the context of Western industrialized nations, the pie is increasingly invisible. These manifestos that at one time captured an awareness of inclusivity in social movement now make me more keenly aware of the dangers of exclusivity and the continual importance of building alliances among social movements that engage us in the task of 'human' liberation.

At the same time as I was collecting these manifestos of 'I', 'We' and 'You', I was also reading and teaching the literature of black psychology (e.g. Jones [1972], 1978). This, as much as the newly emerging feminist literature, was a source of understanding social movements and for thinking about eventual coalition-building. Despite the variety of these manifestos I found that a model set in terms of black race awareness (Hall *et al.* 1972) made sense of them. The model was historically based and empirically tested and made no claims beyond what it studied: primarily university students in the 1970s in the era of the black consciousness movement. Yet, the elements of the model could be found in the developing consciousness of feminists and other marginalized groups.

As I slowly abandoned the idea that theories were value-neutral, I found myself using this model continuously in classes in social psychology where I often taught material from a minority perspective. It was a useful analysis because it acknowledged the emotional basis of social awareness. It described a process whereby personal growth and political engagement were valued as were connections among groups rather than divisiveness between them. The model offered an historical and political dimension to research in social psychology, which from the mid-1970s on had become so irrelevant to the politics of my daily life. I was never able to convince myself through the practice of experimental social psychology that the particulars of culture, nationality, class, gender, race or ethnicity were unimportant to social life and consciousness. If there were general principles of human social behaviour, it made sense to me that they would be rooted in the 'stubborn particulars' of everyday life.

Hall *et al.*'s work (1972) on race awareness provided me some insight into how I had traversed the various elements of developing a feminist consciousness. Their model moved me away from experimental laboratory data and focused me on thinking about 'process', and, in the case of consciousness-raising, a process that would keep changing and taking new forms. Their research pieced the process together through survey and interview methods, through biography, autobiography and all manner of documents, films and novels available to the social psychologist. The model provided a framework for the manifestos I had been collecting. Hall, Cross and Freedle were proposing a model of understanding the change from Negro to Black awareness in America in the late 1960s and early 1970s which I found applicable to an under-standing of the development of feminist awareness. Cross revised the model in a 1978 review paper and continued on with research to support a stage-developmental model of movement towards black awareness.

Cross summarized studies done to validate a model of the 'process of becoming Black' (1978: 81), a model that specified 'the various stages Black Americans traversed in seeking a more authentic identity during the late 1960s and early 1970s' (Cross 1978: 81). He saw this as a model that formulated transformations of identity in adults and that located these transformations in the context of a specific social movement. Although I am white, I found the questions of assimilation versus sepa-ratism that he posed for black identity quite applicable to my emerging feminist identity.

The stages he was able to identify theoretically and empirically predominantly among college students began with a pre-encounter phase in which a black person held a worldview 'dominated by Euro-American determinants' (Cross 1978: 85). This deracinated frame of reference was changed by an 'encounter stage' that 'describes a shocking personal or social event that temporarily dislodges the person from his old world view, making the person receptive (vulnerable) to a new interpretation of his identity and his condition' (Cross 1978: 85). There followed an attempt to make a transition from the old perspective to the 'just discovered Blackness' (Cross 1978: 85). In this phase, white culture is vilified and black culture is deified. (This is, of course, where my manifesto collection seemed to fit best with its sharp divisions of 'us' and 'them'.) Somewhere in this phase, the person became more critical and Cross suggested that 'the most difficult period of nigrescence comes to an end' (Cross 1978: 85). In the next phase of internalization, there was the development of a pluralistic non-racist perspective, less hostility, anxiety, less defensiveness and, in the last stage of commitment, there were those who continued an involvement as social activists on behalf of Black people and all oppressed peoples. This last stage hinged on Cross's notion that 'in order for Black identity change to have *lasting political significance* (his emphasis), the "self" (me or "I") must become or continue to be involved in the resolu-tion of problems shared by the "group" (we)' (Cross 1978: 86). Cross reviewed the considerable support for the model based on a variety of methods of obtaining information: asking black and white students to sort statements reflecting the stages of the model, asking black college students to give retrospective accounts of their Negro-to-Black identity transformation, self-questionnaires, and in-depth interviews with college and non-college participants.[4]

The manifestos I've described and the model of the development of black consciousness coincide with my personal development and they have influenced the way I have come to read social psychology. My propensity to turn things upside down and look at things from multiple perspectives continues to grow. As my social psychology classes begin to reflect the multicultural reality of Canadian society, I find myself talking about multiple perspectives in the construction of social knowledge, social identity and social activism. I am experimenting with techniques by which students might think through multiple accountings for social events and different subject positions for producing knowledge claims about the social world. For the past two years, I have put this issue in the context of producing knowledge about indigenous peoples in Canada since the political events of my country have so focused Canadians on the social psychology of nationhood and intergroup conflict. Both within and between native and non-native groups there are real conflicts over land claims, self-government and the justice system to name but a few areas.

My goal is to have students come to question the kind of non-conscious 'speaking for others' that has emerged in academic social science research and that sustains domination–subordination relations. If I can loosen the grip of the dominant position that sees indigenous peoples as either conquered or extinct by reconnecting with historical and contemporary evidence to the contrary, then I am making way for a social psychology that would foster greater social justice. To that end, students are asked to look at their understanding of indigenous peoples from a variety of social psychological perspectives.

Students were asked first to identify their 'own voice' or perspective. I asked them to write about their own racial and ethnic heritage and how they have personally come to 'know about' native peoples in Canada. For their own perspective, students were asked to reflect but not judge as they become the observers of their social identity formation. I asked them to run a camera back through their lives and let emerge the concrete details of their understanding, a technique common to fiction-writing, psychoanalysis and body/mind meditation practices. I stressed that they did not need to provide the information in a linear and chronological way. The collection of 'episodes' and 'fragments' from family life, school experiences, television, books and friendships revealed how Canadian students (whose origins span the globe) have come by their personal knowledge and social prejudices. It is intended to be a self-study of relative privilege and an exploration of the consequences of privilege for constructing knowledge about others. For native students, it has proven to be an exercise that has elements of the developmental model of self-awareness I have described earlier for African-Americans.

The second perspective required students to take the particulars of their individual experience and to see if concepts in their social psychology text-book – stereotyping, racism, prejudice, inter-group conflict, assimilation, the contact hypothesis – made sense of these experiences. I then asked students to compare insights from social psychology and social history by having them read an essay, 'Stealing history', by one of my colleagues in Canadian Studies, Parker Duchemin (1988). His article connects these general social psychological terms (which he also uses) to the concrete historical reality of colonialism and racism encountered by Native peoples when European settlers arrived. In this way, students can see that the contact experience of Europeans and Native peoples and their subsequent history has shaped consciousness for both groups as well as shaping the kinds of knowledge claims that each group currently makes about the social world. This perspective paves the way for students to re-examine the textbook account of Native peoples they have learned earlier in their lives; it creates a space for alternatives that legitimate the fuller account of the role Native peoples have played in world history (see, for example, Weatherford 1988).

The third perspective for creating knowledge is that of a native person. Students are asked to find material from a native perspective illustrating an aspect of social life. It can be a topic also found in their social psychology textbook (the elderly, socialization of children, conformity, deviance) or missing from their textbook (storytelling, spirituality, connectedness to the land, resistance to oppression). This perspective was the most difficult in that students were often unsure of what constituted 'social psychological knowledge' in another culture. It challenged them to go outside the bounds of personally and/or academically defined ways of understanding social life and to confront the limits of their social scientific understanding and its imposition of academic rules about the structuring of knowledge. Students attended films, plays, exhibits, cere-monies; they brought in poems, stories, songs, newspaper articles, politi-cal documents, and interviews with native friends.[5] They had to discuss the generalizability of this one voice to the many native voices emerging in Canada at this time and similarly the generalizability of their own voice to those of their own background.[6] They had to ask about the rela-tionships between knowledge production and social change – whose perspective will be heard and whose point of view will inform social policy and change?

I have come to take the view that experiments are the stories of main-stream North American social psychology. The analytical voice of acad-emic psychology has something to offer in its conceptual generalizations once grounded in social history, filtered through the voice of 'self' and aware of the longstanding exclusion of epistemic traditions of powerless groups. I have not asked students to choose *the* authentic voice because even within any given social identity there will be conflicting and contradictory perspectives. What I do hope is that they reflect on the question of who has had the power to shape knowledge in the Academy and what have been the implications for consciousness and social change for those historically excluded from speaking on their own behalf.

Chapter 6

One man's social psychology is another woman's social history

You gotta say this for the white race – its self-confidence knows no bounds. Who else could go to a small island in the South Pacific where there's no poverty, no crime, no unemployment, no war and no worry – and call it a 'primitive society'?

(Gregory 1962: 110)

We have looked at how the generation of hypotheses and investigative practices are embedded in the particulars of cultural and temporal context and are further filtered through the 'voices' of individual researchers. The same can be argued in the case of the presentation and interpretation of research findings. Even the best-known research is embedded in the 'stubborn particulars' of time and place which prompts us to question the trans-historical nature of the conclusions drawn from that research. One of the examples of the historically situated aspects of research interpretation involves a well-known study by Leon Festinger, Stanley Schachter and Kurt Back – published in 1950 as a book, *Social Pressures in Informal Groups: A Study of Human Factors in Housing* – and a lesser known piece of research, 'The study of rumour, its origins and spread', published as a journal article in 1948 by Leon Festinger and his associates (Festinger *et al.* 1948, 1950). Both studies took place in American post-Second World War housing projects at a time when housing was scarce.

The first study (referred to as the Westgate study) was conducted in 1946 by the Research Center for Group Dynamics that was then located at the Massachusetts Institute of Technology. The study was commissioned by the Bemis Foundation, which believed that industrialists involved in post-war mass-produced housing could learn from social scientists some of the social factors relevant to creating more than technically sound houses. As stated by the Bemis Foundation's director, 'People may buy houses, but they make them homes, and they live in neighborhoods' (Kelly 1950: vii).

Festinger, however, looked at social psychology as an opportunity to learn about the general processes of social communication. At the time of writing about the Westgate studies, Festinger *et al.* seemed to have two goals in mind. He and his co-authors wrote that 'While the selection of research problems in this study was guided primarily by basic theoretical interests, we do believe that some of our findings should contribute to a better understanding of the phenomena with which many practitioners must deal' (Festinger *et al.* 1950: 178).

In fact, in the published book that followed from the study, 'two outstanding practitioners in the field of housing' (p. 179) were asked to explore the application to housing of the Westgate study and their essays followed the presentation of empirical findings in *Social Pressures in Informal Groups*. However, Festinger's research is not remembered for its application to housing issues but rather for its theorizing about inter-personal attraction and social communication processes within the domain of social psychology.

Some years later in an interview (Patnoe 1988), Festinger spoke differently about the intent of the Westgate studies:

> I have always wanted to go back and forth between laboratory studies and studies in the real world. Field studies, if you will. The field studies were not being done for a practical purpose. They were being done to clarify theory and get hunches ... The Westgate studies have no practical purpose. We did later studies, like *When Prophecy Fails* (Festinger *et al.* 1956) for the same kind of reason. But again, there is no practical orientation, that isn't what fascinates me.
>
> (Patnoe 1988: 255)

What intrigued Festinger about Westgate was the possibility of developing general theories of social behaviour. His work directed social psychology in the 1950s towards abstraction and the study of functional relationships and away from experientially based theorizing. To achieve this goal, he adeptly capitalized on naturally occurring situations in which he could introduce experimentation that might have given his work more applied focus than was his apparent intent. For my purposes, what is significant about the Westgate study is the abstractness of its authors' intent and the questions this poses for research interpretation. When we read the book, the 'subjects' recede into the background and what becomes foremost are the generalized processes of friendship formation, social communication and influence. Schachter, when interviewed by Patnoe (1988), corroborated the importance of theorizing and attested to the decontextualization of the research:

> Leon [Festinger] had a grant to study this housing community called Westgate and we simply got these interviews and combined sociometry with a set of questionnaires. It was presumably to be a study of housing satisfaction which couldn't have interested any of us

less, but it was the basis on which I think the grant was given to him
... [w]e started finding all these nice relationships and took off. That
particular study led to Leon's whole theory of pressures to conformity
and social influence, which in turn led to dissonance.

This group, which was in essence 'Leon's boys,' simply worked out
the whole theory of pressures to uniformity. We each did – starting
from the Westgate book and later theorizing about it – we each did a
thesis related to part of it, which Leon then integrated and had this
rather nice theoretical scheme, which I think, led him into all his other
work.

(Patnoe 1988: 192)

Westgate and Westgate West were new housing projects built just after the
war for married students returning to study at Massachusetts Institute of
Technology (see site plan of Westgate and Westgate West in Figure 6.1).

People moved first into the Westgate project with its '100 pre-fabricated,
single-family houses ... grouped in nine distinct court units' (Festinger
et al. 1950: 15) in the spring of 1946, and the study began in July of that year.
The Westgate project looked as follows (see Figure 6.2).

The occupants were described as a relatively homogeneous group of
'married veteran engineering students' (Festinger *et al.* 1950: 9). Over half
of Westgate's 100 families had small children and it was that central fact
that prompted me to question whose reality this study reflects and how
I might reinterpret the findings.

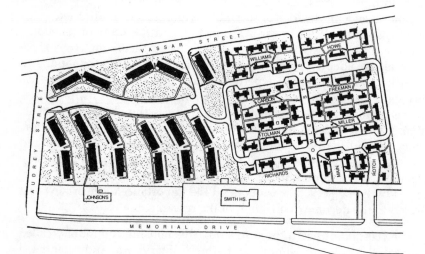

Figure 6.1 Site plan of Westgate and Westgate West
Source: Festinger, Schachter and Back 1950: 14

Figure 6.2 Photographic view of Westgate
Source: Festinger, Schachter and Back 1950

I thought about what a mother of small children would have experienced living in a housing project in which 'the nearest shopping district or store of any considerable size was about two miles away and the closest transportation system, a somewhat erratic trolley and bus line, about 3/8 of a mile distant' (Festinger *et al.* 1950: 14). From the researchers' point of view, this 'relative isolation' was thought to be 'a distinct advantage' (p. 14) for the study. The researchers were interested in how the group influenced individual members and how outside contacts would have less chance to have an impact on the development of relationships given this isolation. But I couldn't stop thinking about what it must have been like for a young mother whose husband was busy with studies to be living in this place.[1]

As I started to read the brief excerpts of interviews with forty women in the project, it occurred to me that I was reading the social history of a particular group of American women whose voices were muted with the domesticity of the late 1940s into the 1950s. In 1946, the respondents were an average age of 26, from upper-middle class backgrounds, who 'had almost all attended college or some kind of professional school' (Festinger *et al.* 1950: 19). They were that generation of American women who might well have raised their families and abandoned their professional aspirations in the post-war era. They were also that generation influenced by the publication of Betty Friedan's *The Feminine Mystique* (1963). Possibly several had abandoned their relatively comfortable lives in favour of some form of starting over in mid-life, be that divorce, remarriage, living alone or re-entering the labour force. If you are in your twenties, they would be the age of your grandmothers, an average age of 74, were all of them still living in 1994. It occurred to me that there was a story here other than the one presented by the researchers, but lost in the abstractness of the language of social psychology as it was then developing.

According to the text, what these women hoped for out of life at the time was to 'own their own homes in the near future . . . with three or more bedrooms . . . in or around a large city' and to have their husbands hold 'successful careers in industry' (Festinger *et al.* 1950: 19–20). While nowhere to be found in the text, Kurt Back, in a later interview, remembered them this way:

> They were all upper middle class kids. The women were rebels because you weren't supposed to get married to a student – somebody who clearly couldn't support you. The women came out in the interviews saying that their mothers were all very upset and would look at where they were living and cry and things like that. Having other couples in the same boat – living below their traditional standard and being attacked by their parents – gave the couples in Westgate a common feeling.
>
> (Back, cited in Patnoe 1988: 74)

It was at this point that I took my fluorescent pink highlighter and worked through my personal copy of the book with a 'gendered' reading of the text. That is, I read the book for what it could tell me about women of that time, not for what it could tell me about the generalized laws of social communication. It was particularly legitimate in this case, because the study was based exclusively on interviews with wives. The researchers tell us their reasoning:

> Since the men were all deeply engrossed in their studies, careers, and part-time jobs, the women of the family usually bore the burden of social life; the women would be easier to contact than the men who were busy in their classes and labs at all hours; to interview the woman in one family and the man in another would almost certainly introduce variables which we could neither control nor identify; to interview the man and woman in each family would have hopelessly complicated the interviewer's task.
>
> (Festinger *et al.* 1950: 226–7)

In all fairness to historical context, at that time the central assumption stated explicitly by these researchers was acceptable in research practice:

> If the data from these interviews are to be taken as giving a picture of the entire community, it is necessary to assume that the family can be reasonably regarded as a unit and that this unit can be studied by interviewing only one of its members ... in all cases that could be checked ... the data obtained from interviewing the wife did adequately give data about the whole family unit.
>
> (Festinger *et al.* 1950: 227)

Indeed, it might be the case that in that era, women made the social contacts not just for themselves and their children but for their husbands. As the authors noted later in the text:

> All the men living in these houses went to the same school and consequently had many opportunities for meeting each other outside the housing project, yet these physical and functional proximity factors operated strongly.
>
> (Festinger *et al.* 1950: 160)

That is to say, when wives were asked 'What three people do you see most of socially?' their responses did not follow a pattern that might be based on the friendships their husbands made at MIT. The pattern was rooted in the community in which these women lived their daily lives.

But let us reject the assumption that wives can represent husbands and see what can be learned about women's social history from *Social Pressures in Informal Groups*. Let us ask how the life circumstances of these women might have affected the formation of friendship groups rather than, or in addition to, simple physical arrangements of houses. What does physical location mean to women? What does it mean to women with and without children?[2] What does 'socially' mean when the following question – 'What three people in Westgate or Westgate West do you see most of socially?' – is asked of women with and without children?

Festinger and his colleagues looked at how small *physical* distances accounted for the formation of friendships through what he called passive contacts. He argued that *functional* distance – for example, where one picks up mail, where there are staircases – also influences the possible contacts and therefore the friendships; but, for the most part, the conclusion is that small distances form the basis of the formation of friendships in homogeneous groups, with the greatest choice being made of next-door neighbours.

A 'gendered' reading of the text takes as its starting point the constraints on women at home with young children. A 'gendered' reading is a challenge to research that interprets findings out of context of the 'particulars' in which the findings are embedded. First, we are told early on that 'the assignment of houses or apartments to particular people had not been made on any kind of selective basis' (Festinger *et al*. 1950: 74). Furthermore, we are told that

> The individuals who moved into this housing project did not choose the court or building in which they would reside. They were assigned to houses in rotation, and after the project was filled initially other occupants moved in only as vacancies occurred without any selection on the part of the new residents.

> (Festinger *et al*. 1950: 174)

However, we know that 'fifty of these one hundred houses were designed for occupancy by married students without children' and that the remaining fifty houses each had an extra bedroom and 'were intended for married students with children' (p. 15). And while a 'first come, first served' principle operated, it was also the case that 'the only expression of preference permitted was between one- and two-bedroom houses' (p. 17). Thus, families could be assigned in rotation without seeming bias, because the bias was already built into the construction of the houses.[3] It can be seen from an enlarged site plan of two Westgate courts (Williams and Howe) which of the houses were intended for married couples with children and which are for couples without children.[4] A schematic diagram of the arrangement of these two courts looked like Figure 6.3.

Researchers at this time obviously did not see the selective gender-linked bias in their study. Since having children or not having them was not considered a 'variable' of any significance to the study of social communication or friendship formation, they could write that there were

Williams   Howe

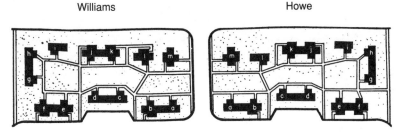

Figure 6.3 Williams and Howe Courts: schematic diagram of the arrangement of
the Westgate Court
Source: Festinger, Schachter and Back 1950: 42

no 'selection' biases operating. Moreover, since friendship choices were
theorized in this research as representative of trans-historical and trans-
situational behaviours, the placement of homes with and without children
would have made little difference in the interpretation of findings.

Yet, looking back one can see that the matter of having children was
very likely of importance. In the matter of friendship formation, we are
told that 'The greatest proportion of possible choices is made to next-door
neighbours' (Festinger *et al.* 1950: 42). This might be so but the choice
is confounded by the fact that there is a greater probability that the
next-door neighbour will be similar to oneself with regard to having
or not having children. While the authors described the layout of each
court as 'identical', from the point of view of having children, this is
not the case. Looking more closely at Williams Court, for example, houses
were assigned a letter, *a* to *m*, and sociometric choices received from
court neighbours were analysed accordingly. As can be seen from
the schematic, houses in any position, *a* to *m*, are not identical with
respect to having or not having children in them and one has a greater
than 50 per cent chance that the next-door neighbour is in similar
circumstances.[5]

I would argue that a 'gendered' reading of the text provides more
evidence that it is the experience of mothers at home with small children
that is central to the meaning of this study. Mothers had to create a
culture of childcare that included an adaptation to lessened mobility and
extreme isolation. In Westgate and Westgate West, women were most
likely to rely on others nearby, in the same court and next door. Small
children increase the probability that one will not stray too far. One
can check on a child or hear her waking from a nap one door away but
that's about as far as one might want to stray. The authors were
perplexed by greater than expected social choices of individuals in the
lower-floor middle apartment (no. 3) from upper-floor residents in
Westgate West. A schematic diagram of a Westgate West building is
provided (Figure 6.4).

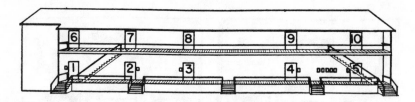

Figure 6.4 Schematic diagram of a Westgate West building
Source: Festinger, Schachter and Back 1950: 36

Looking at the layout of a Westgate West apartment building, it occurred to me that one could understand this finding, again if one took into account the responsibilities of women with small children at play. Mothers with small children might have sat around the staircase outside Apartment 3 watching children play in the area in front of the building, given that there was at this time no formal play area for the children.

My reinterpretation of findings from Westgate and Westgate West suggests that choices of nearby individuals for social contact are influenced by the physical circumstances of having to care for very young children. We cannot ascertain this with any certainty from the data as they were presented. However, given the confounding in the site plan of the Westgate courts and the puzzling choice of Apartment no. 3 in Westgate West, we are at least alerted to a loss of detail that cautions us about interpreting the data out of their context. Rather than interpreting the results as generalized social patterns, I find myself making sense of them as a unique contribution to women's social history.

What else is to be learned about women's lives from this study? From the forty Westgate women, selected at random for interviews in the summer of 1946, parts of two of the transcripts were reported and they provide a more detailed understanding of the life circumstances of women with and without children in the housing project. One woman recounted her experiences as follows:

> My husband wanted to come back to school and being able to find no other place, we came here . . . It's the first place of our own, so we're thrilled about it. What I did like was the idea of having a place of our own and room of her own for the baby. She's never had that before . . . . I think we'll never again have a chance to live in a place like this where everyone has the same interest and everyone is so friendly.
>
> (Festinger *et al.* 1950: 21)

When asked about the difficulties for Westgate women who work, she replied

> Well, I don't work but I would like to. The greatest problem I've heard about from the working girls is shopping. I don't know what else – of

course, trying to get their housework done. For those who'd be willing to leave their children and go to work, it would be wonderful if Tech would set up a nursery.

(Festinger *et al.* 1950: 21)

This woman said she wanted to join a university social club for women (MIT Dames) but 'the meetings aren't at a convenient time' (p. 22). She also said:

I feel we need an organization. Also we ought to have a little place for the girls to gather in the evenings so we don't have to sit here, not saying a word while our husbands study. Just sit! Very few of us know outside friends and we can't invite Westgate friends in while our husbands study.

(Festinger *et al.* 1950: 22)

And of the contacts with neighbours, she said:

[d]uring the day we keep running in and out of the houses – for no excuses, for no reasons, my husband says it's just like living in a dormitory. Then bridge in the evenings – some place close so I can listen to the baby.

(Festinger *et al.* 1950: 22)

This woman was delighted when management seeded the grass and was hoping that they would fix the leaky roofs. She thought complaining as a group might bring better action. She said:

I think a lot could be accomplished by organizing – recreation, nursery, getting things done. The management has been very good but some girls are still lacking pieces in their refrigerators and have iceboxes.

(Festinger *et al.* 1950: 23)

Anticipating the study's results, she mentioned that because of the way the houses were arranged at Westgate 'everyone gets acquainted with the people in their own court' (p. 23). In Westgate, the social hub of activity was the court where most of the women spent their time and social life.

The second interview was from a working woman without children. This woman found people friendly but was looking forward to leaving. Her only tie to Westgate was her husband and her furniture. She told the interviewer that 'the only great difficulty' (p. 24) she experienced holding her job, as a secretary to an insurance man, was shopping. As for involving herself in community activities in Westgate, she said:

It would be hard for anyone who works to talk about that. I just don't have the time. I presume those girls who stay at home would like bridge clubs and teas occasionally. I imagine things like this would serve to bring the wives together especially. I don't know anyone outside this court. Boys seem to get around and know more people ... there is no central meeting place.

(Festinger *et al.* 1950: 25)

Her social contacts were on weekends out on the porch and dinner with her husband's classmates and their wives. These two interviews stand in marked contrast to one another because of one being a woman at home with a child and the other being out working with little time to spare for social activities.

The researchers did not totally overlook the impact of children on the lives of their respondents. They noted that there were restrictions imposed on leisure-time activities by student life and by 'limited finances or having to look after the baby' (p. 30). However, children were not a central focus. They interpreted the circumstances of these women, 'the isolation of the community, their relative maturity in the college community, the absorption in study, the large proportion of families who had small children, generally meager financial resources and congenial neighbours' (p. 30) as contributing factors to the 'modest, though pleasant, manner of life within the community' (p. 30) and to a homogeneity that predisposed people to the influence of ecological factors in friendship formation. The centrality of children was, however, more apparent from descriptions of the community's attempts to organize.

During the period of the study, a tenants' organization was created that did not have the initial strong support of the community. It was spurred on by a fire in a Westgate West building. As described by the authors, 'Men rushed home from their classes ... Westgate came alive that evening. Petitions were circulated through the project requesting M.I.T. to provide fire alarm boxes inside the project ... This was the immediate stimulus to the founding of the organization' (Festinger *et al.* 1950: 62).

About fifty of the 200 people in the Westgate community attended the first meeting. Despite the greater involvement of women in the Westgate community, three men, Rob, Sid and Milt, directed the organization and 'the meeting developed into a somewhat ineffectual discussion, top-heavy with parliamentary procedure' (p. 63). Despite some resistance, meetings continued and twenty projects were started. After Westgate West was completed an invitation was extended to its residents to join the tenants' organization and the purpose of the organization was stated more explicitly: 'Mainly to get better acquainted among ourselves, to set up committees to handle employment for wives (including baby-sitting problems etc.), to act as a unit when making recommendations to M.I.T., and to sponsor social events, sports events, etc.' (Festinger *et al.* 1950: 68–9).

Among the twenty projects undertaken, the four that were dropped, 'a nursery school, a co-op grocery, a community laundry, and a community recreation building' (p. 65), were the very ones that could have facilitated the lives of women at home with small children.[6] Some plans went forward, most of which were social activities, and 'in its four months of existence, the Westgate Council had succeeded in three things – a directory of Westgate, a moderately well attended exercise class, and a block party' (pp. 65–6). It is further noted that 'only a handful of people asked for any help from the employment bureau' (p. 65) which had been set up for Westgate wives. The council was run by a small group of individuals while many others resisted organized activities. It is difficult to know how men and women shared the tasks of the organization, or how they encouraged or interfered with projects relevant to women's lives.

In a section of the book that delineates attitudes towards the Westgate Council, four husband–wife cases are described, two of which provide information on what drew or propelled women to a tenants' organization. For example, Marie L, according to the authors: '[f]elt that this attempt at group action was a valuable experience in the one-sided training for engineers. She was also enthusiastic about the projects the Council could undertake, "everything the members want, laundry, financial aid, nursery school, a cooperative store". . .' (Festinger et al. 1950: 77). Both Marie L and her husband Jack L participated actively in the council as council clerk and a committee chairman respectively. On the other hand, Winnie S did not feel she had time to participate in the council although she was not unfavourable towards it. In keeping with the primacy of children as organizers of women's lives, it was mentioned that she 'kept busy with a vivacious three-year-old daughter' (p. 78). Moreover, the text further specified that, for Winnie S, a friend 'with a child of the same age who lived in a nearby apartment house often came over to have the child play in the yard. She formed few friendships within the project' (Festinger et al. 1950: 78).

From this point on, the text becomes more abstract and mathematized and further removed from the experience of the residents. The authors tested out ideas about sub-group formation and cohesiveness. They offered generalized statements such as 'The more cohesive the group, the more effectively it can influence its members' (p. 100). In statements like this and those that run throughout the remainder of the book, women's experiences in forming friendships and their participation in a tenants' organization are further decontextualized. Despite the use of women's experiences and choices as the data base, the language of 'the group' is used to discuss pressures to uniformity and consequences for deviation, and how rumour is communicated through friendship networks. The authors have already accepted that 'women' will represent the couple, and having done so, they introduce increasingly abstract constructs:

By the use of some of the standard and relatively simple manipula-
tions of matrix algebra we are able to analyze such things as subgroup
formations, cliques, and indirect chains of influence from one person
to another.

(Festinger *et al.* 1950: 133)

In the final chapter, 'A theory of group structure', the language reverts to
the 'generic' male. Statements are made that are not consistent with my
own knowledge of how women, brought together through their common
responsibility for small children, actually experience their lives. For
example,

It is relatively rare that one person, on his own initiative, goes out of
his way to meet someone socially.

People generally hesitate simply to introduce themselves to
someone new. It is only after two people have seen each other several
times that they will start to nod to each other from a distance and only
after some time will it seem appropriate to communicate verbally.

(Festinger *et al.* 1950: 154)

While these statements sound reminiscent of my experience as an
academic in the workplace, they don't sound particularly descriptive of
the experience of women who are thrown together with other women
because of 'having children'.

I take this first study to be about the 'stubborn particulars' of women's
friendships in post-war America. Festinger *et al.*'s slightly earlier study[7]
published in 1948 as 'The study of rumour, its origins and spread' can
also be reinterpreted as a study of women's struggles to organize early
childhood education and daycare. It was intended to be a study of several
aspects of group organization in a low income housing project that had
been built during the war for shipyard workers in Weymouth, south of
Boston. After the war when housing was scarce, the resident profile of the
project began to change.

In 1947, the housing project under study was no longer exclusively
inhabited by shipyard workers. Unemployment was low with the majority
of the men working at skilled labour or supervisory positions. Ninety-
seven per cent of the families had children, with 73 per cent having more
than two children and with 83 per cent of the children under 10 years of
age. There were no nursery or after-school facilities. The research report
tells us that the group felt ashamed of living in low-cost housing and that
a tenants' committee existed that consisted of a few women who were quite
frustrated by failed attempts to organize. Kurt Back described the intent of
the researchers in this way:

It was a downward sort of mobility and nobody felt socially like a
shipyard worker so they hated the place. They tried to make it a whole

community-action research study. Community workers came in and it became this big inchoate kind of research which might have been great but then Lewin died.

Lewin was very involved in the Weymouth study. It was to have been 'the great study'. The idea was to change them, to make them a cohesive group – to make them believe in the group, to believe, 'Our project is good, we have good people here, we can do things, we can communicate'.

(Back, cited in Patnoe 1988: 74)

It is the published article, interpreted through the particulars of gender, that tells us something about women's attempts to organize in historical context. We learn that the community worker/researcher (J. Fleischl) met with a group of five women. These residents were chiefly concerned about developing nursery, school-age recreational and adult educational and recreational facilities. This small group grew to number fifteen women as the intervention progressed. The first general meeting was attended by forty women and three men and plans for developing the above-mentioned concerns were begun. For example, many of the women organized to raise funds for starting a nursery school and for hiring a teacher.

At this point we are told that the researchers wanted to study various aspects of groups but that the women were becoming suspicious of all the experts in their community. It is important to know that the women involved in the organizing in this community were never advised of an ongoing study so they did not know of the dual role – community worker/researcher – that some of the people in their midst played. This proved fatal and might have undermined a potential alliance among women for social action and change. Kurt Back saw the consequences to Festinger and his associated researchers this way: 'The best thing they got out of it was that we were almost kicked out because people thought we were communists. And they wrote one article about rumour' (Back, cited in Patnoe 1988: 75).

A resistance developed to placing children in the nursery school. Two things were clear from the report. First, that the resistance focused on the outsiders or 'experts' and second, that the secretary of the tenants' committee was instrumental in creating some of this backlash. She joined forces with Mr M, described as a 'commy hunter', to accuse another member, Mrs C of being an 'avowed communist' along with some of the outside 'experts'. The nursery school project stopped and community activities were halted. The 'experts' were at a loss to rectify the situation because they had already bypassed the community.

Mrs C, who had done much of the organizing, was linked with one of the community workers and this fuelled the rumour that Mrs C was a communist. It was known that she had dinner at the home of the community worker and it was the latter who had picked out a temporary teacher for the nursery school who was willing to work without pay to help. In a meeting to discuss the nursery school a movie had been shown that had music in it that 'sounded Russian' and when the film projector broke down, it was interpreted as intentionally limiting discussion. Mrs C was scapegoated and only later were matters clarified.

Intended changes in the community never came to fruition but, as Back noted, a published description of the spread of rumour did come about (Festinger *et al.* 1948). The description is equally interesting from a 'gendered' perspective because it reveals the risks to women working collectively in their communities after the Second World War and during the 1950s' period of anti-Communism in American life.

The two studies I have discussed are examples of the caution that must be exercised in the interpretation of research findings. In these studies, the privileged voice is that of the researcher who, through his report to us, has framed our interpretation of the findings as the social psychology of friendship formation and rumour transmission. The researcher's choice to report what happened at Westgate and Weymouth in this way mutes the particular voices in the study. The voices of the women and the disappointment of some in failing to create change in their communities can only be intuited. The interviews with women at the beginning of the text become an abstract and impersonal voice of scientific respectability. A potential source of understanding women's struggle to create social change in the post-war American era is diminished by a seemingly 'scientific' text.

Festinger, Schachter and Back's study of the Westgate housing project (Festinger *et al.* 1950) has been cited over the years primarily for the assertion, provided in Chapter 3 of *Social Pressures in Informal Groups*, that 'the most striking item was the dependence of friendship formation on the mere physical arrangement of the houses. People who lived close to one another became friendly with each other, while people who lived far apart did not' (Festinger *et al.* 1950: 10). While later sections of the text examined the formation of a tenants' association and the spread of rumour within the community, social psychologists tend to report this study for its assertion that physical proximity or propinquity influences attraction and friendship formation. The effect is sometimes explained by the enhanced liking that arises with increases in familiarity to those close by.

As we look back at both these studies in their historical context, the particulars of the research can help us to shift the context in which we might want to make interpretations and systematic generalizations. The shift is from the generic 'subject' to the lives of women. What more do we know or can we find out about the history and development of women's friendships? How do friendships among women differ when we take children and housing arrangements into account? How do class, ethnicity and race interconnect with these factors to limit our abilities to generalize about women as a group? How did women organize in the post-war years to facilitate their children's early education and their own continued education? The two studies that I have discussed are, when viewed from a 'gendered' interpretation, just a glimpse of women's social history although they remain part of mainstream social psychology's decontextualized analysis of interpersonal relationships and social communication.

Chapter 7

Everything I always wanted you to know about . . .

When faced by the textbooks and the journals of social psychology, with their specialized vocabularies and their descriptions of the strange rituals of experimentation, one might ask 'what is the meaning of all this activity?' The answer is not to be found merely by examining the motives, laudable or otherwise, of the practitioners of social psychology; nor is it to be discovered by looking at the stylistic qualities to be found in their discourse. Instead, the argumentative context of social psychology must be sought.

(Billig 1990: 52)

It is generally believed by academics that textbooks exert a powerful influence on students' understanding of psychology. Ziman, in his description of historically different modes of communication in scientific communities, writes that textbooks:

expound currently accepted views, within a standard curriculum, for the benefit of students. An undergraduate textbook that has been recommended widely for a popular course in many universities is a valuable literary property, and comes to exert a wide influence. Its point of view will become established as the conventional wisdom in the subject, the original source of a paradigm from which the next generation of research workers will not easily escape.

(Ziman 1976: 199)

I was reminded recently that the impact of textbooks may not be imme-diate (the time when psychologists often like to measure effects). In a discussion of free trade, an American-born colleague and I somehow arrived at the topic of previous American challenges to Canadian political independence. My colleague began to talk about the time when the Americans won the War of 1812. I didn't remember it that way at all[1] and unearthed my Grade 12 history textbook, McNaught and Cook's (1963) *Canada and the United States: A Modern Study*. I consoled myself with the following: 'By the end of 1814 the war had dragged to a conclu-sion. Clearly, neither side had won. But even a draw was an impressive achievement for Canada, for despite the odds against her, Canadian independence from the United States had been preserved' (McNaught and Cook 1963: 290).

The possibly subtle and slow-acting inculcation of values achieved in the curriculum through textbooks was discussed explicitly at a Canadian symposium in 1978 on the teaching of social psychology. I had returned to Canada in 1977 after graduate work and teaching in the United States and found myself almost completely preoccupied with American social issues and assimilated to American ways of conducting social psychological research. At that symposium, I heard Jim Alcock read a paper on 'Social psychology textbooks and the importation of values'. He argued that 'textbooks, like television, influence the way in which we perceive and interpret our own society' (1978: 2). He went on to say that 'imported social psychology textbooks deprive students of knowledge about their own society' and that through these imported values, 'often taught without conscious awareness by the teacher', 'we may be gradually teaching our students to integrate themselves psychologically with their American neighbours' (1978: 2). Alcock, Carment and Sadava's *Textbook of Social Psychology* (1988) undoubtedly grew out of that symposium and aimed at providing 'a social psychology of Canadian life' by using Canadian content within the American textbook structure.

It is possible to question American political and social ideology conveyed in textbooks of social psychology while setting apart scientific values as inviolable by national concerns. On the other hand, one could tackle the historical development of psychology as a science within American cultural and intellectual practices and the role that textbooks have played in this process. In such an historical perspective, science itself does not escape time and place and the development of textbooks as the central purveyors of scientific knowledge becomes of interest.

My own starting place for understanding textbooks was enhanced by Tom McArthur's *Worlds of Reference: Lexicography, Learning and Language from the Clay Tablet to the Computer*. In the author's view, his book is 'an account of the long effort involved in knowing, and struggling to retain what we think we know' (McArthur 1986: ix), one result of which is the kind of knowledge that we amass in textbooks.

McArthur traces out the 'taxonomic mentality' (1986: 41), that is, the desire to compile everything conceivably thought of as knowledge. He chooses Pliny's *Natural History* in the first century AD as one arguable forerunner to the 'scientific treatise, the monograph, and even the textbook' (1986: 43), by virtue of some of the literary conventions used, namely, clear subject divisions, referencing of sources of information, attempts at objectivity and comprehensiveness. McArthur tells us more about compilers down through the generations and when he gets to the rise of monastic schools in the Middle Ages he reminds us that texts were 'rare and precious' (p. 58) and that this was still an oral culture. Out of the monastic schools developed the centres of general learning, the *studium*, that extended beyond clerical control. A guild for scholars of the studium known as a *universitas* grew up around these centres and eventually 'the name for the scholarly brotherhood was transferred to the institution in and for which they worked' (McArthur 1986: 59).

It is in that milieu that the textbook developed into a unique form of written communication. The textbook required mediation by members of the guild, and McArthur writes:

> [i]t is the teacher who, as mediator, controls the use of the book – and without the teacher the book would not usually be read at all by most of the people for whom it was designed. Its justification is entirely in terms of the institution in which it may be used, the course into which it may fit, and the master or mistress who may use it.
>
> (McArthur 1986: 62)

The textbook was part of the system of oral repetition and debate. Textbooks were read or studied, not just consulted, as in the case of reference works. Textbooks were considered the foundation of a good education and were guarded by the gatekeepers of the universities.

Outside the universities other compilations of the thirteenth century, more like 'teach yourself' books, flourished. From the late fourteenth century on, compilation continued with a vengeance enhanced by the invention of the printing press, the rise of the printing trade and the publishing industry. As European culture moved from its oral tradition to a 'scribal' one, the world of books became a commercial industry no longer monopolized by the Church or the universities. McArthur's 'taxonomic mentality' gave rise to the establishment of various types of reference works: dictionaries, grammars, encyclopedias and the thesaurus.[2]

The textbook genre of scientific communication is altered by the commercialization of books, as well as by the rise of science, popular and academic, and changes in the university as an institution of learning. Diane Paul (1987), in her paper 'The nine lives of discredited data: old textbooks never die – they just get paraphrased', dates a marked change in the university textbook to the 1970s. 'As recently as the 1960s', she writes, 'textbooks tended to be idiosyncratic, reflecting the author's own approach in both style and substance' (Paul 1987: 27). This is consistent with my own findings (Cherry and Corkery 1986) that the conceptual framework for social psychology textbooks became fairly standardized in the mid-1970s, favouring the natural science model over the historical (see Chapter 1 for further detail).

Paul sees the change in textbooks as a response to the 'enrolment surge of the sixties' (1987: 27). It is in this decade that textbooks were simplified for less skilled readers. Publishers introduced ghostwritten or 'managed textbooks' to overcome academic literary habits that didn't market well.

The numbers of textbooks increased. For example, one of the first thorough content analyses of introductory psychology textbooks[5] (Quereshi and Zulli 1975) was conducted on a sample size of seventeen textbooks written or revised between 1968 and 1972. The replication study performed three years later (Quereshi and Sackett 1977) included sixty textbooks written or revised between 1968 and 1975. There were, by mid-1980, about 120 introductory psychology textbooks in print (Rogers and Bowie 1984) claiming to provide authoritative accounts of valid knowledge in psychology. One study of widely used social psychology textbooks found that authors rarely cite the same studies, with the overlap in citations ranging from 7 per cent to 25 per cent (Findley and Cooper 1981).

Book publishing in the United States was a six billion dollar industry by 1980 of which 1.5 billion came from the textbook market. Seventy-five per cent of the total sales of college textbooks is controlled by the ten largest text publishers (Apple 1985). In an effort to profit from growing markets, publishers enhanced their books with visuals such as full-colour photographs and 'boxes' and provided instructors with what Paul (1987) calls 'standard satellite materials'[3] such as test files and study guides.

With the growth of the textbook industry, the balance between economic profit to the publisher/writer team and the intellectual goals of the textbook author to provide a survey of valid knowledge has been discussed in the pages of *Teaching of Psychology* (McKeachie 1976), among other places. Textbooks, more than other forms of scientific communication, currently stand at the juncture of 'the popular' and the 'scholarly' and therein lies both their strength in holding student interest and their weakness in perpetuating an oversimplified and often uncritical stance to scientific knowledge. While textbooks are intended as a comprehensive overview of valid knowledge in the field, they have in actuality been shaped over the past two decades for competition in the marketplace of the 'popular' and the 'up-to-date'.[4]

It is the claim that textbooks are a comprehensive summary of valid psychological knowledge that is being increasingly challenged. Using the broader context of a sociohistorical study of knowledge, the critique of textbooks can be added to current studies of laboratory research practices in psychology (Danziger 1985) and the writing of laboratory research reports (Bazerman 1988). There are three broad aspects to the critique of textbooks that I have discerned through a bibliographic study of articles on textbook knowledge in psychology (Cherry 1989).[5] First, there are several articles that seek inclusion for a specific subdiscipline in introductory textbooks accounts, for example, industrial-organizational psychology and school psychology. Other articles seek inclusion of specific themes, e.g. aging, the family and ethics in research, so that students may approach their study of psychology with a greater sense of the relevance of psychology and their own personal rights.

Second, there are several articles that discuss the total absence and/or bias in existing educational materials of the perspective of groups with low status and power in society. These articles generally critique the treatment of gender, race, age and sexual orientation in pedagogical materials and connect to a wider set of references at all levels of the curriculum, e.g. primary readers and high school textbooks. These papers are a challenge to the assertion that textbooks are comprehensive and valid knowledge by examining the politics of knowledge. They explore the issue of whose knowledge is legitimate and consequently distributed through textbooks.

A third and final set of articles provide research showing inconsistencies between textbook presentations and original research accounts. These historically oriented articles challenge the notion that a textbook is to summarize 'the central facts and theories of a discipline' (Paul 1987) by working directly with the validity of the facts in their social and historical context. Several papers explore the diverse treatment in textbooks of historically controversial topics: sociobiology, Freudian theory, 'Jensenism', 'left-wing rhetoric'. Such papers challenge the idea that psychological science is a cumulative science with well-replicated trans-historical facts, well-defined origins, forefounders and classic studies that mean one thing for all time. Historically based studies provide a strong challenge to the idea that there can ever be a factually perfect or near-perfect psychology textbook or one that is ideologically neutral or value-free (see for example, Finison 1983; Haines and Vaughan 1979; Harris 1979, 1983; Lubek 1993b).

The current concern over textbooks is not that they have a point of view but the uncritical way in which their point of view prevails. Textbooks are embedded in the often unstated values of the textbook writer, the publisher and the larger scientific community. It cannot be assumed that a non-American texbook of social psychology will do anything more than substitute Canadian experiments for American ones while still accepting that textbooks are exemplars of valid social psychological knowledge.

Given the standardization of the natural science approach conveyed in social psychology textbooks over the past twenty years, it becomes increasingly important to place students in a critical rather than an authoritarian relationship to the textbook. There are a variety of ways of doing this. Textbook writers might consider an explicit chapter on the sociological aspects of the production of psychological knowledge in their books (Finison 1983) or instructors might preface the use of the text with such materials. Instructors could involve students in the critical comparison of textbooks. Students might compare versions of a study across several textbooks of the same period, or across different time periods by examining several textbooks or editions of the same textbook over time. I have asked students to trace the changing context in which various studies are located (e.g. Sherif's boys' summer camp studies) and to trace the rise and fall (and rise again) of various themes (e.g. chapters on social movements in social psychology) in order to obtain a broader sociohistorical perspective on what they are studying. Finally, a return to books of original readings in psychology with textbooks consulted as reference works rather than memorized as valid knowledge is more in keeping with a critical stance to knowledge and with the textbook genre at present.

It is however, more likely that North American university students will continue to learn most of the analytical perspective social psychology has to offer through textbooks. The textbook will introduce them to a large set of 'findings' backed up by bracketed references to journal articles but rarely will introductory students read in any depth, a challenge that awaits more senior undergraduate and graduate students. How then to approach the material of social psychology in a way that engages students in the 'argumentative context' of social psychological analysis? For this approach to be taken, the research article needs to be presented as a persuasive communication that constructs its argument through appeal to experiment or survey data. Argument precedes data. By comparing journal articles in pairs, for example, it becomes possible to see the persuasive aspects of social psychological texts more clearly.

One might start by encouraging students to ask questions of journal articles, such as 'What's the story here?', in the same way that they might look at any other instance of cultural communication – rock videos, romance novels, rap songs or virtual realities. What are the multiple purposes served by the journal article for its author and its audiences? This is a way of going beyond the literal story to the meta-narrative, to sensitize oneself to the rhetorical devices used by different modes of communication and to engage in a dialogue with the authors of the articles *as equals*.

This sort of exercise can serve a broader purpose than learning to read critically for the strengths and weaknesses in social psychological research design. It places a further value on questioning the questions framed by social psychologists. North American university students have, for the most part, learned to accept textbook knowledge as a literal representation of reality by the time they begin to read articles in any depth. The multiple-choice and fill-in-the-blank format of testing their knowledge reinforces this notion of single correct answers. Problems that arise are those of experimental design, procedure and statistical analysis but not generally problems of assumption and meaning.

Not unreasonably in a society steeped in meritocratic beliefs, under-graduate students often come to research articles assuming that only the best work is printed for consumption. They have little awareness that before the article ever reaches their eyes, the author has made choices about form and content within the context of a complex set of interconnected social relations. The author will be thinking about several issues not unrelated to the intellectual merit of the research itself. She or he will be constructing the paper according to the publication policies and styles of a particular journal. The author will be aware of which journals are likely to give this research a more sympathetic review. The author will be asking at various points in his or her career whether the journal is regarded as one in good standing in the peer review process for tenure, promotion and other academic rewards.

Where, how and even whether the article that students are reading reaches print is a matter of study in and of itself. In recent years, I have introduced students to the field of social studies of science that is rich with anthropological investigations of investigative practices (Latour and Woolgar 1979). The field includes analyses of how written research reports take shape (Knorr-Cetina 1981; Bazerman 1988). Writing the research article is itself understood as a social activity in which several individuals often participate. Report writers have different statuses and roles (undergraduate researcher, graduate student, junior faculty member, research consultant, senior faculty member) that can affect the control they have over what is included and what is excluded in the research report. In the final decision-making process, the written report is shaped according to stylistic (e.g. third-person narrative) and formal (e.g. sequence of introduction, methods, results, discussion) criteria established by historical convention and disciplinary gatekeeping mechanisms which enforce what is to count as knowledge (Lubek 1993b; Rothman 1971).

In classroom discussions of any social psychological topic, students have their commonsense and often contradictory views of that topic.[6] It is often part of the classroom dynamic to have a general discussion and to hear quite different points of view. This is followed by the professor putting forward the research article or the textbook as the arbiter of these points of view, as in 'Let's look at what the research says'. It is in our teaching practices that research is established as the ultimate judge of whose 'commonsense' point of view will prevail. By selecting research articles or textbooks in pairs one can demonstrate to students that researchers are not above their own incomplete, commonsense and contradictory viewpoints. There too one can find disagreements that cannot be completely resolved by factual evidence because the researchers have approached their problem of interest with quite different assumptions and values right at the outset. If students can analyse the way in which questions are framed in the works of others, the next step is to examine their own operating framework to see what they have included and excluded from their own intellectual analyses.

A quite reasonable goal for those of us teaching social psychology is that our students might find in an historically contextualized social psychology some significant and humane insights that several of its practitioners have had. Leaving the pseudo-scientific baggage aside, I think that many of the observations made by social psychologists can be used effectively to draw students into an ongoing conversation about knowledge, power and social change in their society. The pseudo-science can also be used to advantage to alert students to the way in which social scientists have modelled their practice on a very narrow definition of systematic enquiry. It is important to see how ideas constructed in the service of liberatory efforts can become useful to an ideology of social control. Inevitably, the concerns of social psychology expressed through any one part of the research data base open onto discussions of morality and politics in the practice of a critical social psychology.

Let me give you an example of how research can be presented asking not 'What are the findings of this or that study?', but rather 'How does researcher X want me to think about phenomenon Y?' For this I'll return to the subject of violence towards women, specifically the subject of rape, to provide an example of how authors/researchers interact with readers through the research report to construct an understanding of their subject matter. My approach will be to contrast a view of the journal article as the unbiased or objective report of the latest findings, with the article as a device wherein Researcher X uses a particular format to argue for an understanding of a social phenomenon in a certain way.

To this end I will contrast two papers that came out in the literature at about the same time and that illustrate how two researchers would have us know about rape in somewhat different ways. One was Martha Burt's (1980) article, 'Cultural myths and supports for rape' and the other was Hubert Feild's (1978) article 'Attitudes toward rape: a comparative analysis of police, rapists, crisis counsellors and citizens'. Both articles were published in the *Journal of Personality and Social Psychology*. Publication in the most prestigious journal in the field of social psychology legitimizes rape as a serious scholarly topic and locates an understanding of rape in one of the largest areas of concern to social psychologists – attitude measurement and change.

That both articles under examination are concerned with attitudinal studies of rape reflects a longstanding commonsense belief shared among social psychologists that behaviour is determined causally by our thoughts, feelings and intentions towards objects and/or people. Furthermore, it is believed that there is some stability to these thoughts, feelings and intentions and that better measurement techniques allow us to find a closer fit between what goes on in the mind and action. Both authors want us to know that what we think and feel about rape, the victims of rape and the perpetrators, is expected to be integrally tied to behavioural outcomes such as judging rapists in a legal context or providing help to victims. They locate the importance of their work in the linkage between attitudes and behaviour. Burt writes:

> The burgeoning popular literature on rape ... all points to the importance of stereotypes and myths – defined as prejudicial, stereotyped, or false beliefs about rape, rape victims and rapists – in creating a climate hostile to rape victims.
>
> (Burt 1980: 217)

> The task of preventing rape is tantamount to revamping a significant proportion of our societal values.
>
> (Burt 1980: 229)

> Developing an accurate theoretical understanding of rape attitudes and assaultive behavior will help make social change efforts more effective.
>
> (Burt 1980: 229)

Feild writes of this linkage:

> The perceptions or attitudes of people toward rape are important for understanding not only their reactions to the act itself but also their behaviors concerning the victim and/or offender.
>
> (Feild 1978: 156)

> [m]any programs designed to prevent rape assume that rape is a social/cultural act best deterred by modifying the attitudes or perceptions of rape held by victims, offenders, and members of the criminal justice system.
>
> (Feild 1978: 157)

There is for both researchers, then, an implicit philosophy of knowledge that considers attitudes as the causal determinants of action. Understanding these antecedents would give us a theory of rape. The utility of collecting attitudinal data is that the theory will derive from (in Feild's case) or be tested by (in Burt's case) the data collection process. Scientific work, they both proffer, is about both description and explanation.

Both researchers presented their work as an improvement on the 'popular' and the 'anecdotal' by a move away from such inexact accounts to the concrete quantifiability of attitudes towards rape. Both argued that their work was important because it provided new and more precise information.

There are some immediate problems that arise with the attitude framework argued in this way. First, one could argue back quite convincingly that if quantification provided greater precision, it may have done so by leaving out much important detail in its unneccesarily rigid categorization of respondents' agreements and disagreements to various statements. One could argue that the studies did not really provide much that was newer than the 'burgeoning popular literature' cited by Burt that combined the more journalistic writings of Brownmiller (1975), Clark and Lewis's (1977) detailed study of 'founded and unfounded' rapes according to Metropolitan Toronto Police records, and Griffin's (1971) experiential account of rape from a feminist perspective. For Feild, some of these same references were acknowledged as 'popular' and 'best-selling'. In both cases, there is an uneasy blurring of the reference to 'feminist' and 'popular'. What both these researchers want us to know, however, is that rape understood quantitatively is more accurate than, and an improvement over, rape understood qualitatively, popularly and anecdotally. That's the argumentative structure behind their research and the one with which students need to engage.

It seems reasonable to debate much of what attitudinal research promises us. In this example, both researchers promise us a great deal with their two very different studies – a key to social change, new information, explanation and understanding beyond what other sources can provide. This is to be done through the quantitative study of attitudes. Critiques of attitude research, such as those given by Potter and Wetherell (1987) argue that the aim is futile because the variability of accounts is obscured in attitude measurement studies. One can argue that there is tremendous precision in variability – that is, the collection of details eventually adds up to a clearer picture of the phenomenon of interest in all its complexity. Whatever the case, what falls out of the discussion is a questioning of the assumption that the quantification of what people think and feel is somehow a better form of knowledge than any other possibility.

A second issue raised by locating an account of rape in the context of attitudes and behaviour has to do with the limitations of a framework that relies so heavily on the individual outside a socio-economic framework. The reader/student might want to be cautious in thinking that a specific instance of rape is exclusively the product of the psychological predispositions of the rapist and/or victim or that somehow the study of attitudes will lead to the early identification of rapists. Actions of rape and other forms of violence towards women reflect the opportunity structures in our culture that have permitted those actions – privacy of the home, laws that protect men, support from male peers, economic dependence of women. Social psychologists have not always considered the mutual interaction of structural and psychological frameworks for understanding. These other structural frameworks – legal and economic ones particularly – are at work concurrently with the social psychological level of analysis, and they are as reasonable a framework for understanding specific instances of violence towards women.

Up to this point, both researchers want me to locate the study of rape within an individual attitude–social behaviour framework. Looking now more specifically at the studies themselves and how they construct the analysis of rape attitudes points more at their differences than their similarities. While working within the same general investigative framework of surveying attitudes, these two researchers have chosen to instruct us very differently about rape by constructing quite different content, methods of obtaining data and analyses.

In the case of Burt, we are privy to the social pulse of '598 Minnesota adults, aged 18 years and over' (Burt 1980: 220) who accepted to be interviewed by 'experienced women recruited from U.S. Census Bureau interviewers in Minnesota' (p. 220) about their 'attitudes and feelings about the behavior of men and women towards each other in their everyday lives, and also their romantic and sexual behavior' (pp. 220–1). The interviewers indicate also that they are 'particularly interested in what you think about rape and sexual assault' (p. 221). We don't know how many refused to be interviewed from the published article. In the case of Feild we hear from 1,448 (82 per cent) of the surveyed respondents identified as 'adult citizens of a medium-sized community', 'patrol police officers of two urban and two rural communities', 'committed rapists at a state mental hospital' and 'female counsellors from rape crisis centres located in 12 major metropolitan areas across the United States' (Feild 1978: 158). Feild tells us that 'black and white experimenters of both sexes with various levels of status (professor to undergraduate student) were used in administering the instruments' (p. 160) and that they were trained to do so. Some respondents received the inventories individually and others in small groups and all completed the questionnaire anonymously. In the one case, our account of rape comes from relatively intimate one-to-one interviews and in another from more distanced and anonymous survey interactions.

Besides creating a different social context for examining rape attitudes, each researcher has set up the data for quite different analytic purposes. For Burt this takes the form of a regression analysis that shows the way in which various attitudes are weighted and interrelated:

> The research reported here presented a unique opportunity to assess the predictive validity of feminist theoretical ideas about the rape-supportive nature of American culture.
>
> (Burt 1980: 228)

> [T]he author knows of no other published research that attempts to document the complex web of attitudes and beliefs surrounding rape in this culture. The present research, therefore, constitutes a first effort to provide an empirical foundation for a combination of social

psychological and feminist theoretical analysis of rape attitudes and their antecedents.

(Burt 1980: 229)

For Feild this goal takes the form of dimensionalizing attitudes to rape through factor analytic procedures and comparing dimensions across populations. He writes:

Such research is needed for the further development of a theory of rape.

(Feild 1978: 157)

For the most part, when rape attitudes have been studied, the data base has been restricted to anecdotal events or case histories . . . Of course, these data are useful, but such information is not readily susceptible to quantitative analysis and provides little objective evidence on the generality or magnitude of the problem.

(Feild 1978: 157)

There are other quite striking differences beyond who will tell us their attitudes, by what investigative practice and how these attitudes will be structured to provide a picture of rape. The authors themselves turn out to have quite different ideas about what constitutes a rape attitude. In comparing feminist and social psychological research, Lott wrote that 'values are an integral part of science, that they influence all phases of the process, and that they should be acknowledged and made explicit in the same way that we recognize that scientific truths are not independent of time and place' (1985: 159). What then, are the values explicit in these two papers?

First, the acknowledgement of an experiential data base is clearer in Burt's work: 'The present author used feminist writing plus her own extensive field experience with rape victims, victim support workers, and audience response to public presentations about rape attitudes and beliefs to conceptually isolate three additional variables' (Burt 1980: 218). These sources are in addition to and no less important than established findings from 'social psychological research on reactions to victims' and 'literature on the socialization of aggression' (Burt 1980: 217). This researcher blends the personal, political and professional sources of information available to her. There is a sense of personal engagement with the material, whereas in Feild's work there is a clear sense that rape, 'one of the most rapidly increasing, hotly debated, and newly researched crimes in America' (Feild 1978: 157), provides a convenient set of fresh materials to try out ideas about dimensionalizing attitudes through factor analytic techniques. There is no reference to other than 'scientific' commitments.

Burt's work is addressed to what she calls 'rape culture' (p. 219). Consequently, she selects out some statements about rape and tells us quite definitely at the outset that these are 'myths', that is, the stereotyped and prejudiced aspects of beliefs. Burt's 'rape myths' are Feild's 'beliefs or opinions about rape'. Each of the following scale items are roughly comparable:

BURT (RAPE MYTHS)	FEILD (RAPE ATTITUDES)
Any female can get raped.	A woman can be raped against her will.
Any healthy woman can successfully resist a rapist if she really wants to.	A woman should be responsible for preventing her own rape.
Many women have an unconscious wish to be raped, and may then unconsciously set up a situation in which they are likely to be attacked.	Most women secretly desire to be raped.
(Burt 1980: 223)	(Feild 1978: 159)

Burt's language leaves little doubt that rape myths are falsehoods. Feild's approach allows for the possibility that some statements about rape, such as those provided above, are 'beliefs' whereas others are 'factual', that is, some are true or verifiable while others are open to debate. The split between fact and value is a major distinction in Feild's approach to the extent that it is concretized in two separate scales – Attitudes Toward Rape and the Rape Knowledge Test. Feild expresses doubts about his own distinction, one which Burt does not even attempt to concretize in her research. Her approach to the matter is put succinctly: 'Excessive violence has long been a theme in American life; rape is only one of its modes of expression' (Burt 1980: 228), and many of the attitudinal dimensions she explores 'have helped to produce a rape rate in the United States that is the highest of any industrialized country' (Burt 1980: 228).

To find out about attitudes and to develop an instrument capable of assessing attitudes, Feild writes, '[s]ince no published, empirically developed measure of attitudes toward rape was available, the Attitudes Toward Rape questionnaire, or ATR, was developed for use in the study' (Feild 1978: 158). He further notes: 'The content should be indicative of comments or statements frequently cited in the literature as reflecting people's beliefs or opinions about rape' (Feild 1978: 158). His major sources for categorizing domains of attitudes to rape, rape victims and rapists, are, as noted earlier, the popular and scholarly literature, some of which is to be found in recent feminist writings.

Feild goes on to develop an additional measure called the Rape Knowledge Test (RKT). This is a multiple-choice measure of 'people's factual knowledge of rape' (Feild 1978: 159). In other words, Feild separates items according to whether they are expressions of value, opinion or attitude, as opposed to expressions of knowledge.

Even though Feild admits that the 'facts' of rape might be distorted owing to data reflecting biased samples of incarcerated rapists, police reports and reports from victims, he still goes on to construct a test which is guided by his conceptualization that there are factual and non-factual items about rape. The facts of rape for his purposes include 'only items dealing with factual information and verified by two or more independent studies' (Feild 1978: 159). These independent studies are essentially previous social science surveys or police records. Out of a possible fourteen 'correct' answers, the average for the sample was 4.59, indicating that the accounts of rape based on current statistical sources such as the Uniform Crime Reports are not widely known. Furthermore, police records are known to err in the direction of the underestimation of 'founded' rape (Clark and Lewis 1977). It seems untenable to maintain a distinction between factual and attitudinal information in the way that Feild does for a variety of items, given that rape reporting has always been subject to local variation and bears an underestimated relationship to actual occurrence.

Even if one accepted an arbitrary standard of the current factual understanding of rape at any given time or place, it is still not clear whether a respondent in giving information is providing his or her knowledge or opinion. Feild attempts to distinguish what a respondent knows about reported rape from his or her opinions about rape by structuring the former as questions in multiple-choice format with one correct answer and the latter by six-point Likert scales to which there is no right answer but only a scale of agreement or disagreement. Perhaps some examples of the content of items from these scales without regard to Likert versus multiple-choice format would be helpful here. About which items would you be expressing an opinion and for which ones do you have a right or wrong answer? On what evidence are you basing your response?

Reported rapists generally brutalize their victims.
Most women secretly desire to be raped.
The reason most rapists commit rape is for sex.
The percentage of raped women who know their rapist.
Most reported rapes occur in the victim's residence.

Feild completes his study by relating the attitude (ATR) and knowledge (RKT) instruments to his respondents' attitudes towards women, various demographic features of the sample, and finally to the extent of contact respondents have had with victims of rape and rapists. This particular study of rape attitudes wants us to know about rape as a concretization of previous popular and scholarly writings. The concrete attitudes are separated into those which are 'factual' and those which are attitudinal, with only a footnote indicating the possible limitations of this division.

The study by Burt also begins with the aim of providing a delineation of rape attitudes and takes the perspective that rape myths are part of a broader nexus of attitudes. It is the interrelationship that is important, that is the interconnectedness of beliefs about the nature of rape, rapists and victims. These additional attitudinal variables include sex-role stereotyping, sexual conservatism, adversarial sexual beliefs and the acceptance of interpersonal violence. From this quite different starting point, Burt has not separated fact and value in designing a set of response items. She has drawn on both the popular and academic literature as well as her own quite extensive experience in the field of rape prevention.

These authors want us to know somewhat different things about rape attitudes despite using a similar attitude–behaviour framework. Burt wants us to know that rape myths are only part of an interconnected set of ideas contributing to rape culture. Feild wants us to separate the facts of rape from beliefs and to think of the latter in terms of dimensions that he finds 'make sense' quantitatively and confirm the available literature.

Burt is conducting her data-gathering exercise to direct it outwards towards efforts at social change. She writes:

> The data reported here imply that changing adherence to rape myths will not be easily accomplished, since they are so closely interconnected with other strongly held and pervasive attitudes.
>
> Developing an accurate theoretical understanding of rape attitudes and assaultive behavior will help make social change efforts more effective.
>
> (Burt 1980: 229)

Feild strikes me as more concerned with finding a 'relatively objective way for measuring concepts not previously well "operationalized"' and to improving 'the psychometric properties of the scale'. He writes:

> The ATR (attitudes to rape) . . . might be applied to any investigation in which the assessment of rape attitudes could play an important role.
>
> The present data are thus presented as a tentative model, albeit crude, in the hope that future research on rape attitudes might be stimulated.
>
> (Feild 1978: 177)

When I present students with these two 'understandings of rape' there is inevitably a discussion of their own different understandings of violence towards women. Conflicts arise as to who defines what is rape? Many of the women students feel the space opened to discuss feminist research on rape that leads into discussions of the differential perceptions of men and women in our society. Often we spend considerable time debating the usefulness of studying attitudes outside of a social, legal and political change paradigm. Ideally, whether it is a textbook or a journal article that students read next, they will think it reasonable to ask 'What's the story here?' and 'How does this researcher want me to think?'

Chapter 8

Lost in translation

Research is . . . an informal, messy-looking process. It is so different from the stereotype that it has even been suggested – somewhat facetiously – that the history of science be rated X (Brush 1974) and kept from impressionable young students because it does such violence to the image of scientists as careful weighers of evidence pro and con, concerned only with being objective. The most important parts of research are, in fact, subjective and have little to do with elaborate quantitative analyses or expensive laboratory equipment. The essential components of research – where it begins and where it leads – have to do with observations of phenomena and the development of hunches, ideas, and questions about the hows and whys of things.

(Jones, R. 1985: 3)

Well over a decade ago, I started to return to the social psychological research that had captured my imagination as an undergraduate in the 1960s. First on my list was a study by Muzafer Sherif and his associates on conflict between two groups of boys at a summer camp in Oklahoma, as it had a very personal appeal for me. I had attended a summer camp in my early teens and a string of rainy days must have prompted the counsellors to think about how they were going to manage an increasingly unruly set of campers who were beginning to factionalize and turn on counsellors and one another. (Either that or we were unwittingly participating in someone's research study!) Whatever the case, they came up with a plan to unite us.

We were told that a madman had escaped from a nearby asylum and that we would all have to cooperate and band together to make sure no harm came to anyone. We were fed together, housed in the main dining area rather than in our separate cabins and sent out on walks together in common search of the madman. I may well have been the only camper who reported seeing him in the woods wearing a plaid shirt, a sighting that turned out to be one of the great humiliations of my life when we were told that it was all a hoax. When I came across the Robbers' Cave study in my introductory social psychology class, I remembered my anger at being manipulated by our counsellors despite their good intentions to keep campers from making each others' and their lives miserable.

I returned to the boys' summer camp studies (Sherif *et al.* 1961) in a more systematic[1] fashion shortly after I heard a colloquium Ben Harris gave at Carleton University in the 1979-80 academic year. I was motivated to look again at the Robbers' Cave experiment just as Harris (1979) had with John Watson and Rosalie Rayner's 'classic' study of Albert and conditioned fear (Watson and Rayner 1920) to see if the reporting of the research had become systematically transformed over the years or whether this activity was something unique to the career of Watson. If there were 'origin myths' and transformations in social psychology's construction of its past, I was curious to know what themes operated in the telling of the field's history?

Harris had concluded in his research that 'most accounts of Watson and Rayner's research with Albert feature as much fabrication and distortion as they do fact' (Harris 1979: 151). He cited several reasons for this, namely the reliance placed on secondary sources by textbook authors and their desire to make experimental evidence consistent with contemporary theories, an attempt to make Watson more credible to students coming into the field of psychology, and finally Watson's own active participation in changing the description of the original study. Harris' perspective on the 'Little Albert' research was that the matter was one of psychological mythology and provided a good example of aspects of the sociological dimensions of science.

Harris's research warned that one should be wary of secondhand accounts of psychological research, particularly classic studies, but one should also examine further the process 'by which secondary sources themselves come to err in their description of classic studies' (Harris 1979: 157). Harris was chiefly preoccupied with how classic studies come to shape the origin myths of a discipline and to build into a discipline a 'false sense of continuity'. Harris noted that origin myths are not intentionally fraudulent but rather a part of the extra-scientific world that shapes a particular discipline. Rejoinders to Harris asked 'How typical is the Little Albert case in the history of rereporting psychological research?' (Cornwell *et al.* 1980). These authors wondered 'How many other notable experiments have multiple originals?' Harris saw more in the 'Little Albert' scenario than a cautionary tale and proposed building 'a socially informed, critical history of psychology' by examining the political and social context within which psychology developed. He put his emphasis less on the biographical and personal intentions of individual psychologists and more on the social forces that shaped the seemingly 'linear' recording of the discipline's development.

This approach is quite important in writing a critical history of social psychology. The practice of social psychology has developed within both academic sociology and psychology. It has been shaped by behaviourism, psychoanalysis, evolutionary theory and field theory. Its practices have fluctuated with the extra-scientific political climate of the times in ways demonstrable through historical research (see Collier *et al.* 1991 in general; see Bramel and Friend 1981; Samelson 1980 and 1986 more specifically).

In social psychology there are numerous examples of classic studies: Asch's studies of conformity and independence, Milgram's studies of obedience, to name but two lines of inquiry. These are studies that have given researchers a way of conversing with one another in a common vocabulary. They delimit the field for incoming students and provide a 'sense' of tradition from a point of origin. A classic study is used to mark the origin by signalling a break with a previous tradition: for example, Triplett's demonstration of social influence marks the movement of social psychology beyond philosophical speculation or archival evidence into a scientific realm, by virtue of its use of experimentation. Scientific rigour is claimed and a sense of cumulative progress from the classic study onwards can be charted.

By the time I came to learn about the Robbers' Cave study it was well on its way to being a 'classic'. Those who wrote about it thought about it in this way – as a memorable and ground-breaking piece of research. While it was most often cited in the 1950s and 1960s textbooks in chapters on intergroup conflict and prejudice, it was also cited as an example of international and organizational conflict.

By the mid-1970s the Robbers' Cave study was often seen as a classic in methodology with less emphasis on the content. Textbook authors in social psychology variously referred to Sherif's research as 'ground-breaking work', 'the now classic Robbers' Cave experiment', 'the elegant field experiments' and a 'justifiably famous experiment'. In this sense of 'classic' the study combined sociological description of groups in a field setting with the laboratory methods more often found in general psychology at a time when research methods were playing an important role in defining disciplinary boundaries. The study showed that experimentation could be woven into everyday life with as little suspicion as in the laboratory.

The Robbers' Cave Study can be considered 'classic' as an idea with wide applications to fields other than the original group used in the research. While conflict among eleven-year-old boys at summer camps served as a convenient starting place, once extrapolated to conflict among adults in large organizations, among ethnic and racial groups and on the international level, the ideas have more wide-ranging appeal and approximate the rhetoric of those sought-after universal laws of social behaviour. Robbers' Cave is also a classic in a more narrative sense – it is a memorable story documenting a deeply felt hope of many social scientists (and liberal thinkers more generally) of the post-Second World War era that social arrangements could be created whereby human beings could reach peaceful rather than violent ends.

As I began my research I wanted to know how this particular classic study compared with Harris's analysis of the mythological proportions of Little Albert? To do this, I looked first at the possibility of multiple originals. What became apparent when I looked more closely into the 'classic Robbers' Cave experiment' is that there were three summer camp studies. While Robbers' Cave is better cited and remembered it is the last of a series of experiments with groups of boys at summer camps, each of which had its own unique features. Here are the details of each of the studies.

Date of study	Location	Names of groups of boys
1949	Connecticut	Bull Dogs and Red Devils
1953	Upstate New York	Panthers and Pythons
1954	Robbers' Cave, Oklahoma	Rattlers and Eagles

The texts that can be considered 'originals' – that is, the texts where the findings of each of the three studies can be found – indicate that there were also multiple originals. These are as follows:

Rohrer, J.H. and Sherif, M. (1951) *Social Psychology at the Crossroads*, New York: Harper and Bros (Chapter 17 contains the 1949 study).

Sherif, M. and Sherif, C. W. (1953) *Groups in Harmony and Tension. An Integration of Studies in Intergroup Relations*, New York: Harper and Bros (Chapters 9 and 10 contain the 1949 study).

Sherif, M. (1954) 'Integrating field work and laboratory work in small group research', *American Sociological Review* 19, 759–71 (contains summaries of 1949 and 1953 studies).

Sherif, M., Harvey, O.J., White, B.J., Hood, W.R. and Sherif, C.W. (1954) 'Study of positive and negative intergroup attitudes between experimentally produced groups', Robbers' Cave Study, University of Oklahoma, Norman, Oklahoma (multilith containing part of 1954 study).

Sherif, M., White, B.J. and Harvey, O.J. (1955) 'Status relations in experimentally produced groups through judgemental indices', *American Journal of Sociology* 50, 370–9 (reports the hand-toss experiment from the 1953 study).

Sherif, M. (1956) 'Experiments in group conflict', *Scientific American* 195(5) (Scientific Offprint #454 contains a composite of 1949, 1953, 1954 studies).

Sherif, M. and Sherif, C.W. (1956) *An Outline of Social Psychology*, New York: Harper and Bros (2nd edn, presents 1949 and 1953 studies in Chapter 6; contains 1954 study in Chapter 9).

Sherif, M. (1958) 'Superordinate goals in the reduction of conflict', *American Journal of Sociology* 63, 349–56 (contains part of the 1954 study).

Sherif, M., Harvey, O.J., White, B.J., Hood, W.R. and Sherif, C.W. (1961) *Intergroup Conflict and Cooperation. The Robbers' Cave Experiment*, publication of the Institute of Group Relations, Norman, Oklahoma, 1961. (presents *ASR* paper, Chapter 1; contains the multilith of 1954 as Chapter 2).

Sherif, M. (1967) *Social Interaction: Process and Products*, Chicago: Aldine Publishing (contains the 1954 multilith as Chapter 22).

Sherif, M. and Sherif, C.W. (1969) *An Outline of Social Psychology*, New York: Harper and Row (3rd edn contains 1949, 1953, 1954 study results in Chapter 11).

Sherif, C.W. (1976) *Orientation in Social Psychology*, New York: Harper and Row (contains 1954 study in Chapter 5).

Unlike accounts of the Little Albert study, the details provided in each of the accounts of the boys' summer camp studies are quite similar. In subsequent accounts by social psychology textbook authors, there are minor errors that confuse details of the studies, for example, the names of the groups, the exact location of the camps, the types of tasks required by campers or the procedures for assigning the boys to groups (i.e. random assignment vs. carefully matching). For the most part, the sequence of successive stages in each of the intergroup experiments is described consistently in each of the originals and Table 8.1 highlights the similarities and differences among the studies.

Table 8.1 Stages and activities for each of the intergroup studies (I=Connecticut; II=Upstate New York; III=Robbers' Cave Oklahoma)

Stage of experiment	Experiment		
	I	II	III
In-group formation			
Spontaneous interpersonal choices		X	X
Arbitrary division into two matched sets according to specific criteria	X	X	X
Intergroup conflict			
Win–lose competition	X	X	X
Planned frustration of in-groups	X	X	
Reduction of conflict			
Common enemy, individual activities, adult intervention	X		
Contact without interdependence	X		X
Series of superordinate goals			X

Source: Table 11.1 from Sherif, M. and Sherif, C.W. (1969) *Social Psychology*, 3rd edn, New York: Harper & Row. Reprinted with permission of HarperCollins, New York. Copyright© 1969.

In his writings Muzafer Sherif often described the three studies as a progression from the first to the third where, by the last study, intergroup conflict was reduced to a greater extent than in the first two studies. He located the research in terms of his previous work on norm formation linked to an interest in conflict and cooperation between groups. More generally, Sherif saw the 'common threads' of his work as research that could have bearing on 'actualities', that could address a 'significant persistent problem in human affairs', and that selected methods according to the dictates of the problem in question (Sherif, M. 1967: 8). He wrote of the personal background for the common themes in his work in this way:

> As an adolescent with a great deal of curiosity about things, I saw the effects of war: families who lost their men and dislocations of human beings. I saw hunger. I saw people killed on my side of national affiliation; I saw people killed on the other side. In fact, it was a miracle that I was not killed along with hundreds of other civilians who happened to be near one of the invasion points the day Izmir (Smyrna) was occupied by an army, with the blessing of the victorious Western colonial powers at the end of World War I . . .
>
> I was profoundly affected as a young boy when I witnessed the serious business of transaction between human groups. It influenced me deeply to see each group with a selfless degree of comradeship within its bounds and a correspondingly intense degree of animosity, destructiveness, and vindictiveness toward the detested outgroup – their behavior characterized by compassion and prejudice, heights of self-sacrifice, and bestial destructiveness. At that early age I decided to devote my life to studying and understanding the causes of these things. Of course for some years I did not know how to go about it, but I started reading whatever I could lay my hands on about history and social problems. By the time I came to the United States for graduate study, I had firmly decided that my life's work would be social psychology . . .
>
> (Sherif, M. 1967: 9)

Muzafer Sherif's wife and colleague, C.W. Sherif, elaborated in her textbook, *Orientation in Social Psychology*, on her personal context for the research reflecting the superordinate goal of raising a family, combining two careers, and living a marriage of two cultural backgrounds. In keeping with the intent of her book to tell students about 'how research happens', she described how the summer camp experiments came about. She wrote:

> Any research worth doing starts with questions or a puzzle that plagues the researcher . . . Surely it is no accident that these particular

experiments on intergroup relations should take shape in the mind of a Turkish social psychologist in the United States as the conflagrations and tragedies of World War II smouldered, who had married an American. We were keenly aware that our marriage was an intergroup affair. Had we not been, we would have soon learned.

(C.W. Sherif 1976: 115)

While there is general consistency in Muzafer Sherif's accountings of his work, once the studies make their way into the lore of social psychology the context for describing them often changes to suit the textbook author's point of view. The finding that superordinate goals can reduce conflict between groups, which is only found in the 1954 Robbers' Cave experiment, can be found in chapters on prejudice and discrimination, social change, war and peace and in the introductory chapter of a textbook as a classic in experimentation. As I traced these studies through more than seventy textbooks of social psychology I found that authors generally discussed the more elaborate and successful Robbers' Cave study of 1954 leaving out the earlier studies of 1949 and 1953 altogether. It was the finding of cooperation that was to live on rather than the more dismal message of the first two studies, where the two groups of boys joined in a larger unit to fight a common enemy, be that another group of boys in the first study, or, as I found out in my research, the experimenters themselves in the second study. The 'happy ending' study prevailed despite Sherif's appreciation of social relations as 'messy, contradictory, and fraught with conflict, suffering, and agony' (Sherif, M. 1967: 9).

What strikes me as I reread all three studies is that there was no more reason to valorize the third experiment than the first two. The world is made up of all the outcomes seen in these studies and it has been for quite extra-scientific reasons that the third study – reduction of conflict through superordinate goals – has prevailed in the historical record. The collective writings of the Sherifs speak to our common humanity. Their writings, while acknowledging horrendous intergroup events, are framed with optimism about the ability to transcend human difference to achieve our common humanity. In the era of cold war thinking, with its language of tough-talking deterrence, the Sherifs were bringing an optimistic and liberatory message that people could get along and work for common goals if the conditions were right.

I remember being drawn to their optimistic message. It was quite consistent with much of the liberal social science I met up with as an undergraduate in the late 1960s. North American social psychology, in particular, stressed the malleability of a person's social behaviour. Humans were not locked into fixed destinies but were able to discover and potentially transform the environmental pressures weighing on them. While the extreme downside of this was to be found in Milgram's obedience to authority experiments, one could see the other side in Muzafer Sherif's third study of cooperation among boys at a summer camp. If some of the literature of social psychology confronted the human being with his or her foibles – conformity for no good reason; biased, faulty and irrational reasoning most of the time – one could look to the human potential for cooperation in the Robbers' Cave study. It was a narrative of archetypal transformation from individual selfishness to collective social growth.

What kept my perspective about the summer camp studies in balance was the theoretical work of Michael Billig. Sometime in the course of my research on these studies in the mid-1980s I came across his analysis of the three studies that led credence to another way of thinking about them. It is worth repeating at length (the fuller treatment is in his book, *Social Psychology and Intergroup Relations* (1976)). Billig was concerned with the way in which false consciousness is maintained in subordinate groups to the advantage of dominant groups. When he came to analyse the summer camp studies, he saw not two groups of boys, but three groups of people, that is, two groups of boys and one group of experimenters (camp staff and researchers). He acknowledged that Sherif himself did not want to reduce intergroup problems to individual personality or attitudinal problems but emphasized the 'importance of studying the relations between groups over and above their own internal properties' (Billig 1976: 302). Like so many social scientists, Billig expressed his admiration for the boys' summer camp studies in his own way:

> The research itself is a veritable *tour de force* and an important landmark in social psychological research into intergroup relations. The richness of the results, as well as Sherif's own methodological skill and organisation, ensure that the research will bear re-examination and re-interpretation.
>
> (Billig 1976: 302)

What Billig added that was unique was a different theoretical framework, one that saw the interaction as being among three groups rather than two. He speculated that if the boys, who, he argued, were competitive well before they were given 'experience with competition', were to have found out that the camp was an experiment, they would have behaved quite differently. He reread the studies as three-way group interactions in which one group (experimenters) created a scenario for two other less powerful groups (the boys). Billig succinctly summarized the crux of the three experiments. He noted that in the first two experiments, the boys were brought to camp, became acquainted and were split into groups wherein features of in-group behaviour were noted. Opportunities for competition were arranged wherein out-group antagonisms appeared. In the third experiment, the members of the artificially created hostile groups were presented with superordinate goals that facilitated inter-group cooperation and diminished intergroup hostility somewhat. Not as much, I would add, as textbook authors have claimed in their romanti-cized versions of these studies and not as much as many of us would like to believe is possible in conflict settings.

Billig aimed 'at progressing beyond Sherif's analysis' (Billig 1976: 305) and he did so by asking 'under what objective social conditions do groups subjectively develop superordinate and competitive goals. In short, what relations are there between group beliefs and goals and the objective situations in which groups find themselves?' (p. 306). His answer to this question of whose interest the institution of competitive and/or superordinate goals served resulted in the following analysis:

> One has to face one of the most glaring, and yet neglected features of the whole situation: the one group in the boys' camp with a definite vested interest in the institution of competition and the 'semi-institution' of group cooperation was, in fact neither of the two groups of boys. It was the third group – the experimenters/camp authorities. . . . This third group, the experimenters, is the social group which creates the other two groups – giving them their social meaning and their social reality. This group constitutes the legitimate authority in the camp.
>
> (Billig 1976: 307)

In the descriptive re-analysis of the studies that followed, Billig showed just how often the group of 'authorities' intervened to keep the boys from coming to blows. His detailed analysis showed just how orchestrated competition and cooperation can often be in groups where there is a powerful majority group in charge of less powerful 'minority' groups fighting with one another. Billig went further to state that:

> organised competitions do not arise in some sort of social vacuum, but are created by specific people or groups in specific situations. In the case of the boys' camp experiments, the simplistic explanation would state that the authority group created the competition and this in turn gave rise to the resulting intergroup hostility.
>
> (Billig 1976: 310)

For Billig the more complex analysis involved going beyond the manip-ulation of superordinate goals to achieve harmony between groups. Rather, he wanted to look at the real authority third parties have – managers, world economic powers, privileged groups of all sorts – in setting the goals and creating false consciousness for less privileged groups. In this regard, he concluded that one must return in the boys' summer camp experiments to a wider context of power relations among three parties in the form of 'the original distinction between the camp authorities and the boy subjects'.

Billig went on to suggest that the two groups of boys did not see the dominant group (the authorities) as the source of their intergroup hostility, despite the fact that the conflicts were arranged by these authorities. The ups and downs of the conflicts between the two subordinate groups in the three experiments never altered their relationship to the dominant group. True? False.

Without benefit of archival material and relying on only one 'original' for the second study in 1953, Billig posed the following question:

> whether the groups would have behaved in the same way, would have developed the same ingroup and outgroup perceptions, and would have unquestionably accepted the authority of the camp leaders, had they been aware of the experimenters' intentions and manipulations. Although this is an empirical question for which there is no immediate data, one can ask it with reference to particular features in the experiments. For instance, one can wonder whether the behaviour of the boys would have been different, if they had known that after stage one the authorities were deliberately splitting up close friends – and they were doing this to see whether these friends would turn on each other.
>
> (Billig 1976: 318)

Billig's reinterpretation was borne out by information provided by the Sherifs in the second edition of their social psychology textbook, *An Outline of Social Psychology* (1956), which was replaced in 1969 with a third edition.[2] The reference is obscure and Billig appears not to have known that the boys in Study Two did figure out that they were being manipulated, and staged a mutiny. Tucked away in a footnote in one of the 'originals', I found the following reason given for ending the 1953 experiment in Stage Two: 'In the 1953 study, this stage was not completed. In a frustration episode, the subjects attributed the plan to the camp administration. Since testing hypotheses required that the source of frustration be attributed to the experimental outgroup, the 1953 study was terminated at this point' (Sherif and Sherif 1956: 311).

In other accounts the matter is stated differently. For example, earlier on, in another 'original' Sherif wrote about the 1953 experiment as a failed attempt at integrating field and laboratory research:

> The scope of the experiment embodying laboratory-type procedures at crucial points in each stage proved to be too great for a single attempt. During the period of intergroup relations (Stage III), the study was terminated as an experiment due to various difficulties and unfavorable conditions, including errors of judgment in the directing of the experiment.
>
> (Sherif, M. 1954: 769)

In a more popular 'original' in *Scientific American* published in 1956, Sherif wrote a composite analysis of the three summer camp studies. Here he wrote that 'None of the boys was aware that he was part of an experiment on group relations' and he emphasized that the researchers 'set up projects which were so interesting and attractive that the boys plunged into them enthusiastically without suspecting that they might be test situations'. It is this version that prevails in subsequent writings about the studies, contradicted only by the lonely footnote cited above in a 1956 textbook that was, as mentioned previously, replaced in 1969 with a third edition.

There are several outcomes in these three experiments – each one pointing to the enormous difficulties groups have in working towards cooperative goals. Study One ends with the two groups of boys banding together against a common enemy. Study Two ends with the two groups turning on the authorities who are manipulating them. Study Three ends with the two groups achieving a reduction of hostility through coopera- tive goals being 'arranged' by the authorities. Each outcome is possible and plausible. Study Two is far more interesting in some ways, particu- larly given Billig's theoretical reinterpetation. Yet, it is rarely found in textbooks referencing intergroup conflict.

Our textbook practices of citing 'classics' that fit with prevailing politi- cal notions of the time relegate other less 'successful' studies to the empirical graveyard as 'failures to replicate' or not quite what the researcher is wanting to demonstrate. Billig's detailed analysis of Study Two addressed the issue of what happens in intergroup situations where groups do not have equal power. This is much more often the real world case in the workplace and on the international scene – both areas to which Sherif wanted to generalize. After reading his work and completing a search through all the 'originals' I found myself re-oriented to these studies. Like Billig, I wasn't taking exception to Sherif's methods or to the axiom that experimenters have powerful effects. We need our textbooks to report all the summer camp studies so that the difficult struggles of survival between groups are not lost in translation but posed directly to those who might dream up new ways to find common ground and continue the Sherifs' project of enlarging the 'we'.

These studies signal to me the deeply subjective and important affinity between the researcher and all aspects of the research process: theoretical framework, investigative method, analysis of the findings and the communication of the results across generations of students. It continues to trouble me that when we package and shape social psychology as a scientific discipline that purports to study individuals and groups, we smooth over the mess that has historically existed and still exists in the field. We diminish meaning and understanding. Something is lost in translation. We homogenize, make diversity and conflict vanish and come up with something like a bunch of statements that are meant to mimic 'universal laws' of social behaviour rather than case studies of struggles between differently advantaged groups. There are historical, political, and moral aspects underlying all that we do in social psychology and it seems to me that making those features of our work explicit makes those of us who teach and write social psychology an active part of transforming the social world rather than detached observers of it.

Current research and pedagogical materials in experimental social psychology place a greater emphasis on scientific credibility than political and historical understanding. Through its development in North America from the 1930s to the present, social psychology became the experimental study of individuals in interpersonal rather than collective situations. Standard textbooks continue to give us the contemporary view – social psychology is best conceptualized within the natural science approach through experimentation, quantification and statistical models. Imagine a social psychology grounded in the 'stubborn particulars' of time, place and the lives of people who practise research and social analysis. It would start to tell us more about the origins and changing nature of social inequalities; more about the basis for conflicting perspectives relevant to understanding social problems; and more about the ameliorative effects of different types of social action. This would require teaching and studying social psychology in ways that balance the seemingly individual way lives are often lived with the collective vested interests that each of us brings to the study of social issues but which sometimes remain invisible to awareness.

For me, practising a social psychology grounded in historical particulars continually raises self-contradictions and conflicts. My critical perspective comes from asking not 'What is *the* history of social psychology?', but 'How is social psychological knowledge constructed at different times in the history of the discipline and in whose interest is the knowledge constructed?' It comes from asking questions like these:

Why do textbooks have compassionately written chapters on discrimination against minorities rather than chapters on unearned privileges of dominant groups?

Why have experimentation and quantitative measurement become the hallmarks of social psychology in one culture and not in another?

What are the cultural assumptions in the theories we are reading about in social psychology textbooks? Assumptions about race, gender, class, sexual orientation among other social and political identities.

What happens if I trace a classic study through several generations (editions) of the same textbook or in different textbooks over a given period? Does the recounting of the study change over time or with different authors and if so how can I account for these changes? (Try using the citation index to see how secondary sources reference these studies.)

What ever happened to the study of language or social movements in psychological social psychology? When do they appear in textbooks, when do they disappear? Where do they go?

What's the difference between the study of peace and the study of conflict resolution? What's the story about 'peace' in social psychology's involvement through two world wars and other regional conflicts?

As more of these questions are answered, it will become possible to construct a course in social psychology that begins with the historical context for its development within the field of psychology (as well as sociology). Eventually, a much broader cultural analysis of how 'the social' has been constructed in psychological social psychology will emerge to provide us with a socially informed and transformative project. Less will be lost in translation as our image of the social psychologist and social psychological research becomes more sensitive to conflicts of interest and contradictory perspectives.

Notes

1 ARE YOU A 'REAL' SCIENTIST?

1 The author wishes to thank Harvard University Archives for permission to cite unpublished work from the Allport papers. The conference paper that Allport presented in 1966 was part of the first international Conference on Graduate Education in Social Psychology. It was held in New York City, 16–18 December, under the auspices of the National Science Foundation and the Division of Personality and Social Psychology of the American Psychological Association.

2 The terminology of historical terms – for example, presentism – follows that used most recently in a review article by Hilgard et al. (1991). I am indebted to the participants in my graduate seminar in the History of Social Psychology, Spring term 1990 who were assigned the task of comparing 'histories' of social psychology: Manuel Arango, Anna Chapman, Mindi Foster, Susan Galloway, Lena Ghanotakis, Bat-Ami Klejner, Barbara McLellan, Ian Nicholson and Kimberly Noels. Their papers helped me refine further the way I look at the discipline of social psychology. I am particularly grateful to Dr Betty Bayer who enlivened our discussion and brought Graumann's (1988) history to my attention. Also included in our analysis was Hilgard's history, 'Social psychology', Chapter 16 in Psychology in America (Hilgard 1987).

3 Ian Lubek's (1993a) very detailed analysis of the multiple types of histories and historiographies of social psychology also examines Allport's several Handbook chapters. Lubek observes that their contrast with Allport's 'Six decades of social psychology' paper may have much to do with their intended audiences: a 'textbook' history to legitimate traditional views and a conference presentation proposing changes to graduate education in social psychology.

4 The details of Lewin's invitation to Iowa and how that influenced his whole way of doing research is examined in Mitchell Ash's (1992) 'Cultural contexts and scientific change in psychology: Kurt Lewin in Iowa', American Psychologist 47, 198–207.

5 Parts of this section are based on Ellen Corkery's BA Honours thesis undertaken at Carleton University in 1986 as well as a conference presentation by F. Cherry and E. Corkery (1986).

6 An excellent example of the impossibility of separating the measuring instrument from what is measured that I have presented to students with some success can be found in Lewis Brandt's book Psychologists Caught (1982: 70). The example involves a lengthy illustration of the indeterminate measurement of the temperature of water in a glass with a thermometer. I like to compare and contrast it with an example of the human measuring instrument that

can be found in Schlossberg's (1973) book, *Einstein and Beckett*. John Unterecker's 'Foreword' to that book is cited in the beginning of Chapter 4 of this book.

7 A more detailed analysis of textbook prefaces as persuasive communications is made by Peter Stringer. He analyses the impossible task textbook authors face in 'producing a simple, coherent text' (Stringer 1990: 23), and references numerous examples from standard social psychology textbooks published between 1976 and 1981.

2 KITTY GENOVESE AND CULTURALLY EMBEDDED THEORIZING

1 This essay developed over a ten-year period and is still, to my mind, an example of the unfinished business of theorizing in the human sciences. Many of the ideas were helped along by a sabbatical year (1981–82) spent with Erika Apfelbaum and Ian Lubek at the Social Psychology Laboratory, University of Paris (VII) and by the careful reading of my colleague Warren Thorngate.

2 Some experimental social psychologists have used the language of deductive science more explicitly. For example, Brown (1986) in his *Social Psychology. The Second Edition*, instructs his readers that 'understanding means being able to deduce particular phenomena from general laws, including some phenomena never yet experienced . . .' (Brown 1986: 18). 'Theorizing in terms of social forces – by analogy with social forces such as light, sound, gravity, and magnetism – is an old and honorable tradition in social psychology, associated most closely with the work of Kurt Lewin' (Brown 1986: 18).

3 In generating theories to explain the world around us, it is important not to lose sight of patterns of disciplinary constraints and practices (Sherif, C.W. 1979). The post-Second World War training of North American experimental social psychologists encouraged decontextualization. The general experimental psychologists dominating departments of psychology in the 1950s would have found a social psychology embedded in culture more appropriate to sociology departments where, indeed, interpretive traditions of social analysis did emerge. Social psychologists' training in psychology departments were guided by behaviourism and by a more mechanistic and ahistorical philosophy of science outlined in Chapter 1.

4 Had violence towards women been a central issue in the 1960s, we might have found that reflected in subsequent studies. What seems clearer (with the gift of hindsight and with a view of social psychology as a post-dictive science rather than a predictive one) is the relevance of the Genovese incident to society's increasing confrontation with a continuum of violence directed against women in society, and the failure of institutions and individuals to intervene in such instances.

5 The framework of seeing variables over persons focused researchers on quantitatively measurable behaviours. Once having decided that the behaviour of interest was 'intervening', then we could work backwards to ask which variables altered rates of 'intervening' behaviour. The influence of gender re-entered the problem as an arbitrary way of classifying individuals by their sex, which might be significant depending on its weight in a multivariate computational matrix. Latané's (1981) Law of Social Impact is the covering law that explains variation in bystander behaviour. Race, class and sex are determiners of the strength of social impact rather than code names for how various members of society experience historically created structures of inequality.

6 I want to argue that decontextualization goes on in all social science methodologies, not just laboratory experimentation. I make this point largely because
   it is fashionable to single out only experiments as deterrents to meaningful
   social data. However, any abstraction process, of which all research partakes,
   is subject to the constraints of stripping away important aspects of the social
   context in which the phenomenon occurred. Experimentation, perhaps more
   than other tools of analysis, is the most context-stripping by the way in which
   variables are defined for laboratory use. Since these two studies in the 1970s,
   two highly realistic field studies have been brought to my attention by
   Penelope McGregor, a Carleton University student. Schreiber (1979) found that
   two of 105 onlookers intervened to assist the victim in a staged murder. Most
   onlookers froze. Harari *et al.* (1985) found high rates of intervention (85 per cent
   in groups; 65 per cent alone) in a staged sexual assault of a white woman by a
   white male.

7 While much was written in other newspapers, I chose to see how the paper that
   broke the story continued to keep it before the public. Undoubtedly, more
   could be written from an historical and media perspective. I have included a
   partial list of newspaper accounts and trial summaries consulted. Articles cited
   from the *New York Times* (*NYT*) and the *New York Times Magazine* (*NYTM*):

   'Queens woman is stabbed to death in front of home', *NYT*, 14 March 1964,
     26: 4.
   '37 who saw murder didn't call the police. Apathy at stabbing of Queens
     woman shocks inspector', *NYT*, 27 March 1964, 1: 4, 5, 6; 38: 1, 2, 3.
   'Apathy is puzzle in Queens killing. Behavioral specialists hard put to
     explain witnesses' failure to call police. Interpretations vary. Some say
     tendency not to get involved is typical – others call it uncommon', *NYT*, 28
     March 1964, 21: 1; 40: 1, 2.
   'What kind of people are we?', *NYT*, 28 March 1964, 18: 2.
   Letters to the *Times*:
   'TV called factor in slaying apathy. Psychiatrist gives views on witnesses in
     Queens', *NYT*, 12 April 1964, 66: 3, 4.
   'Apathy discussed', *NYT*, 31 March 1964, 34: 5; 1 April 1964, 38: 6; 2 April
     1964, 32: 5, 6; 3 April 1964, 32: 5, 6; 7 April 1964, 34: 5, 6. *NYTM*: 17 May
     1964, VI, 22; 24 May 1964, VI, 62.
   'Study of the sickness called apathy', *NYTM*, 3 May 1964, VI, 24, 66, 69, 72.
     (A.M. Rosenthal)
   'Trial begins in Queens slaying. Some of 38 witnesses to testify', *NYT*, 9 June
     1964, 41: 6, 7.
   'Moseley recalls three Queens killings', *NYT*, 11 June 1964, 30: 1.
   'Moseley gets chair; verdict is cheered', *NYT*, 16 June 1964, 1: 6; 53: 2, 3.
   'Genovese slayer wins life sentence in appeal', *NYT*, 2 June 1967, 37: 1–5.
   'Genovese slayer escapes on way to Attica prison', *NYT*, 19 March 1968,
     49: 1.
   'Genovese killer is hunted widely', *NYT*, 20 March 1968, 35: 1, 2.
   'Genovese slayer yields gun, gives up. Genovese slayer is seized in Buffalo',
     NYT, 22 March 1968, 1: 3; 39: 6, 7, 8.
   'Moseley back in custody, wants new try at freedom', *NYT*, 23 March 1968,
     22: 2.
   'Inquiry sought in Buffalo case against Moseley's rape victim', *NYT*, 3 April
     1968, 16: 4, 5.
   'Hostage held captive by Moseley in Buffalo inquiry', *NYT*, 23 April 1968, 30:
     4–8.
   'Genovese murderer gets college degree', *NYT*, 10 April 1977, 30: 4.

'Today I'm a man who wants to be an asset', *NYT*, 16 April 1977, 25: 3.

'Convict rehabilitation: unconvincing evidence', *NYT*, 28 April 1977, 28: 4.

'20 years after the murder of Kitty Genovese: the question remains: why?', *NYT*, 12 March 1984, II B1: 1–6; B4: 3–6.

'It's not Kitty Genovese again', *NYT*, 19 December 1984, I 27: 1, 2, 3.

'The 39th witness', *NYT*, 12 February 1987, I 31: 1, 2, 3. (A.M. Rosenthal)

Court cases cited:

The People of the State of New York v. Winston Moseley, Defendant. 251 New York Supplement, 2d Series, pp. 552–6, 6 July 1964 (43 MISC2d505).

The People of the State of New York v. Winston Moseley, Appellant. 281 New York Supplement, 2d Series, pp. 762–7, 1 June 1967 (20 NY. 2d 64).

8 Murder, not rape, is the central aspect of Moseley's criminal actions despite his inclusion in *Against Our Will*. I would encourage reading together, as I did, Brownmiller's (1975) chapter 'A question of race' and Angela Davis' critique of Brownmiller's work 'Rape, racism and the myth of the black rapist' in Davis (1981). Neither author speaks of Moseley's choice of victim in a racial context but their discussion alerts us to the fact that there are dimensions of race and racism in this story that require analysis. Historically and currently racial differences have figured prominently and differently in the lives of whites and blacks. How these differences play themselves out in our daily lives is the task of social psychological analysis. More recent articles are helpful in showing us that race/sex/class are not historically separable in considerations of rape. See Valerie Smith's 'Split affinities: The case of interracial rape', in M. Hirsch and E.F. Keller (eds) (1990) *Conflicts in Feminism*, London: Routledge, and bell hooks's (1990) essay 'Reflections on race and sex' in *Yearning: Race, Gender and Cultural Politics*, Toronto: Between the Lines.

3 STRUGGLING WITH THEORY AND THEORETICAL STRUGGLES

1 Portions of this paper were given at the annual meeting of the Canadian Psychological Association, Calgary, June 1991, at a joint session of the Sections on History and Philosophy of Psychology, Women and Psychology and Social Psychology.

2 Following the Montreal massacre, details of Lepine's life were made public. Feminists working with women victimized by violence were not surprised to learn of the pattern of wife and child-battering that Lepine's father had inflicted on the family.

3 Many of these reasons are consistent with J. Macaulay's (1985) incisive analysis of experimental social psychology's approach to the study of aggression. She also provides a more detailed description of the traditional 'teacher–shocking–student script' that constitutes the experimental study of aggression.

4 Many of these developments are anticipated by bell hooks (1984) in her book *Feminist Theory: From Margin to Center*, particularly in her essay, 'Men: comrades in struggle'. For more details on the work described below, contact Rick Goodwin, PO Box 4465, Station E, Ottawa, Canada K15 5B4.

5 Some years ago, I presented a paper on the interconnection of sex, race and class in the social psychology of second-language acquisition to an interdisciplinary conference on social psychology and language (Cherry 1980). The Bristol conference brought together the only social psychological forum I could find outside a women's studies forum where one could talk about gender, class and race in personal and social identity terms rather than as classification

variables in a regression analysis. Anthony Kroch (1979) delivered a paper on social class and language. In reporting his studies of speech in Philadelphia, he gave a wonderful account of the obstacles of getting in the front doors of patrician Philadelphia homes. Social class had bestowed the privilege of silence and privacy on his potential respondents. What similar difficulties confront us in establishing a psychology of men? Social research is predominantly a phenomenon of the middle class looking at itself or the working or unemployed classes. This leaves us uninformed about the experiences of those with a modicum of privilege except as they choose to share that knowledge.

4 HARDENING OF THE CATEGORIES AND OTHER AILMENTS

1 The re-analysis of Lynn and De Palma Cross' data (1974) formed part of Karen Duncan's Honours thesis (1980) and part of a paper we co-authored for a symposium on 'Gender and Expectations' at the (1980) annual meetings of the Canadian Psychological Association, June, Calgary.

5 SELF-INVESTIGATING CONSCIOUSNESS FROM DIFFERENT POINTS OF VIEW

1 Many of my own experiences were corroborated in an exploratory study that interviewed nine women who identified themselves as feminists. See 'The development of a feminist consciousness in women', a paper presented at the Annual Meeting of the Canadian Psychological Association, 31 May 1990, Ottawa and available from the authors: Nancy Wilkinson and Margaret Schneider, Ontario Institute for Studies in Education, Department of Applied Psychology, 252 Bloor St W, Toronto, Ontario.

2 In classes on prejudice and discrimination, I have used these documents along with first-person narratives of the impact of prejudice and first-person accounts of those who stood up against discrimination, for example, Horacio Lewis's *I Might as Well Move to the Moon* (1972), a detailed account of his efforts to obtain housing despite discrimination, and Daniel Braithewaite's *The Banning of the Book* Little Black Sambo *from the Toronto Public Schools* (1956), a personal account of his successful efforts in 1954 to remove a book that he considered damaging to his children and their efforts to learn in an environment respectful of black children. (This publication is available through Third World Books & Crafts Inc., 942 Bathurst St, Toronto, Ontario, M5R 3G5.)

3 A more extensive analysis of these and other manifestos was undertaken by Cheryl Bryce as part of her Honours thesis (1980), 'Manifestos: an expression of group awareness', at Carleton University. For a more detailed historical treatment of Burris' Fourth World Manifesto, see Alice Echols' *'Daring to be Bad': Radical Feminism in America, 1967–75*, pp. 245–7 specifically.

4 Cross (1991) has extended this model in his recent book, *Shades of Black: Diversity in African-American Identity*, in which he has further explored 'the development of various Black identities – nationalist, bicultural, and multicultural – including Afrocentricity'.

5 One student attended a sculpture exhibit and used an Inuit stonecarving. She asked if it was sufficient to describe it and the expression of living with nature it exemplified. I suggested that she look perhaps for something the carver had written about the sculpture. I realized almost as soon as I said it that I had privileged the printed text and again I had to think through the impact of this kind of biasing in social psychological knowledge construction.

6 I have recently had two students with combined European and Native ancestries tell me about their reconnections to their Native ancestry. Both of them found the narrative technique required by this assignment helpful in focusing them on their struggles with multiple identities. One student is enrolling in a Native teacher's training programme and the other is becoming more involved in the University's aboriginal students' centre. Again, I have been reminded of Cross's developmental model of consciousness by which we affirm our social identity and political commitments.

6 ONE MAN'S SOCIAL PSYCHOLOGY IS ANOTHER WOMAN'S SOCIAL HISTORY

1 In thinking about this study I was undoubtedly influenced by my own experience as a single parent arriving in a new community with a four-month-old child several years earlier. With little social support and a tremendous feeling of isolation, I called on the nearest people with children, the neighbours across the street. At the time of writing, I was thinking also about all of the research I had read over the years on the enormous impact of children on their caretakers and more personally about Meredith Luce, my friends' child whose birth prompted significant changes in lifestyle and housing arrangements.
2 I am particularly grateful to my colleague, Suzanne Mackenzie, Department of Geography, Carleton University who brought to my attention the work of Jacqueline Tivers, *Women Attached: The Daily Lives of Women with Young Children* (1985). Tivers cites extensive data on the home visiting activity of women with small children and her findings confirmed my sense that Festinger *et al.* (1950) required a gendered reading.
3 The text tells us that 'the design and construction of these projects were performed under the supervision of architects in the School of Architecture at M.I.T.' (Festinger *et al.* 1950: 14).
4 I am grateful to Dr Kurt Back who helped me discern houses that were accessible to families with and without children. By examining Figure 6.3, one can see that houses with children have an extra room. A fuller description of the houses is to be found in the text (Festinger *et al.* 1950: 15) where it is indicated that houses without children are two-and-a-half rooms and houses with children are four rooms.
5 The sequence of houses in Williams Court beginning with House *a* (lower right) and moving to House *m* (upper right) is as follows: No Child (NC), Child (C), NC, NC, C, C, NC, NC, NC, C, C, C, C. Courts are not identical with respect to sequence. The letters *a* to *m* were used in the original analyses of friendship choices and are retained here for purposes of discussing their occupancy with respect to children.
6 After completion of the study period, several projects were funded through other sources. However, it is not reported which ones were made possible through alternative funding.
7 The published study is part of a larger unpublished monograph by L. Festinger and H.H. Kelly (1951) entitled *Changing Attitudes through Social Contact: An Experimental Study of a Housing Project*, Research Center for Group Dynamics, Institute for Social Research, University of Michigan, Ann Arbor. The longer version is well worth re-reading both from the point of view of gender and class. I have kept my comments focused on gender only for pedagogical reasons, when in fact both studies together could easily provide more insights into class-based aspects of women's lives.

7 EVERYTHING I ALWAYS WANTED YOU TO KNOW ABOUT . . .

1 Our conversation seems like quaint colonial chit-chat when one considers that modern 'Canada' did not exist as such in 1812 and that the war(s) under discussion were between British colonialists and Americans over territory inhabited and claimed by Iroquois peoples. Were we to rewrite my Grade 12 history textbook from the perspective of the Iroquois nations, for example, we would see the War of 1812 as one part of the long history of devastation inflicted on aboriginal peoples in the Americas (Wright 1992). We might have a very different perspective on who 'won' the war considering the contemporary resistance of Mohawk peoples to further incursions on their lands (e.g. the 1990 resistance at Kanasatake in Quebec).

2 McArthur's final chapters are about the possibilities for reference works once the computer (mathematical calculation) is thoroughly connected to literary compilations.

3 This chapter is based in part on my paper, 'The textbook genre: an overview of its place in the knowledge industry', presented in a Symposium on 'Textbooks in Psychology', given at the annual meeting of the Canadian Psychological Association, 8–10 June 1989, Halifax, Nova Scotia. During the course of the conference at which this paper was presented, 'satellite material' was brought to my attention and deserves special mention as an example of popularization. A representative of Scott-Foresman was present to promote that publisher's introductory psychology text, which includes a history of events in psychology set in a *Time* magazine format.

4 Part of the impact of textbooks comes from the use of the impersonal voice to express authority that transcends the individual writer(s) (Olson 1980).

5 The bibliography on which my conclusions are based is available on request. The list of articles was compiled in several ways: a search of all volumes of *Teaching of Psychology* up to 1986, a follow-up of references arising from this procedure, and a computer search through the following databases: ERIC, PSYCHINFO, PSYCHALERT, SOCIAL SCIENCES CITATION INDEX, SOCIOLOGICAL ABSTRACTS. The computer search strategy used the terms TEXTBOOK(S) with SEX*/AGE/AGING/ETHNICITY/RACE/GENDER/BIAS/DISCRIMINATION/ STEREOTYP*/OMISSION*/IDEOLOGY/ERROR* (*indicates a truncated variable). I am grateful to Ms Wendy Sinclair and Ms Marci Jacklin, Reader Services MacOdrum Library, Carleton University for assisting me with the on-line search.

6 One of the most helpful discussions of the approach social psychology has taken to commonsense is to be found in the writings of Michael Billig, for example, 'Rhetoric of social psychology', in Parker and Shotter (1990).

8 LOST IN TRANSLATION

1 I am grateful to the Social Sciences and Humanities Research Council for support with this research (Grant Number 410–83–1279–R2). I would also like to thank Bruce Baskerville and Sheila Evans for their valuable research asssistance.

2 The first edition of *An Outline of Social Psychology* was published by M. Sherif in 1948, before the summer camp studies were done. Furthermore, in a citation analysis looking at references to the 'originals' between 1973 and 1984, one finds that Sherif *et al.* (1961) is the main source of information for the summer camp studies. There are 172 citations to this source in the eleven-year period

while the 1956 and 1969 textbooks receive fifty-five and 150 citations respectively, not all of which are citations to the chapters describing the summer camp studies.

References

Albin, R.S. (1977) 'Psychological studies of rape', *Signs* 3: 423–35.

Alcock, J.E. (1978) 'Social psychology and the importation of values', paper given at the Symposium on the Teaching of Social Psychology in Canada, Canadian Psychological Association, Ottawa, June.

Alcock, J.E., Carment, D.W. and Sadava, S.W. (1988) *A Textbook of Social Psychology*, Scarborough, Ontario: Prentice-Hall Canada.

Allport, G. (1954) 'The historical background of modern social psychology', in G. Lindzey (ed.) *Handbook of Social Psychology*, Reading, Ma.: Addison-Wesley.

——(1966) 'Six decades of social psychology', unpublished manuscript, Harvard University Archives, Allport Papers, Papers Relating to Lectures, Addresses, Publications, Box 5, File 132.

——(1968a) 'The historical background of modern social psychology', in G. Lindzey and E. Aronson (eds) *Handbook of Social Psychology*, 2nd edn, Reading, Ma.: Addison-Wesley.

——(1968b) 'Six decades of social psychology', in S. Lundstedt (ed.) *Higher Education in Social Psychology*, Cleveland: Case Western Reserve University Press.

——(1985) 'The historical background of modern social psychology', in G. Lindzey and E. Aronson (eds) *Handbook of Social Psychology*, 3rd edn, New York: Random House.

Apfelbaum, E. (1986) 'Prolegomena for a history of social psychology: Some hypotheses concerning its emergence in the twentieth century and its raison d'être', in K.S. Larsen (ed.) *Dialectics and Ideology in Psychology*, Norwood, N.J.: Ablex.

Apfelbaum, E. and Lubek, I. (1983) 'Setting human violence into its historical and socio-psychological contexts', paper given at Understanding Human Violence: An Interdisciplinary Conference on Violence in the Individual, The Portman Clinic, London, September.

Apple, M.W. (1985) 'The culture and commerce of the textbook', *Journal of Curriculum Studies* 17: 147–62.

Ash, M. (1992) 'Cultural contexts and scientific change in psychology: Kurt Lewin in Iowa', *American Psychologist* 47: 198–207.

Bazerman, C. (1988) *Shaping Written Communication: The Genre and Activity of the Experimental Article in Science*, Madison: University of Wisconsin Press.

Bem, S. (1974) 'The measurement of psychological androgyny', *Journal of Consulting and Clinical Psychology* 42: 155–62.

——(1983) 'Gender schema theory and its implications for child development', *Signs* 8: 598–616.

Bem, S. and Bem, D. (1970) 'Training the woman to know her place: The power of the nonconscious ideology', in M.H. Garskof (ed.) *Roles Women Play: Readings toward Women's Liberation*, Belmont, Ca.: Brooks Cole.

Billig, M. (1976) *Social Psychology and Intergroup Relations*, London: Academic Press.

——(1990) 'Rhetoric of social psychology', in I. Parker and J. Shotter (eds) *Deconstructing Social Psychology*, London: Routledge.

Bird, C. (1940) *Social Psychology*, New York: Appleton-Century Co., Inc.

Borofsky, G., Stollak, G. and Messé, L. (1971) 'Bystander reactions to physical assault: Sex differences in reactions to physical assault', *Journal of Experimental Social Psychology* 7: 313–18.

Bradley, B. (1989) *Visions of Infancy*, Cambridge: Polity Press.

Braithewaite, D. (1956) *The Banning of the Book* Little Black Sambo *from the Toronto Public Schools*, Toronto: Third World Books.

Bramel, D. and Friend, R. (1981) 'Hawthorne, the myth of the docile worker, and class bias in psychology', *American Psychologist* 36: 867–78.

Brandt, L. (1982) *Psychologists Caught*, Toronto: University of Toronto Press.

Brod, H. (1987) 'A case for men's studies', in M.S. Kimmel (ed.) *Changing Men: New Directions in Research on Men and Masculinity*, Newbury Park, Ca.: Sage Publications, Inc.

Brown, R. (1986) *Social Psychology. The Second Edition*, New York: The Free Press.

Brownmiller, S. (1975) *Against Our Will: Men, Women and Rape*, New York: Simon and Schuster.

Brush, S. (1974) 'Should the history of science be rated X?', *Science* 183: 1164–72.

Bryce, C. (1980) 'Manifestos: An expression of group awareness', unpublished BA Honours thesis, Carleton University.

Burgess, A.W. and Holmstrom, L.L. (1974) 'Rape trauma syndrome', *American Journal of Psychiatry* 131: 981–6.

Burris, B. (1971) 'The Fourth World manifesto', in A. Koedt, E. Levine and A. Rapone (eds) *A Radical Feminism*, New York: Quadrangle Press.

Burt, M.R. (1980) 'Cultural myths and supports for rape', *Journal of Personality and Social Psychology* 38: 217–30.

Chabram-Dernersesian, A. (1992) 'I throw punches for my race, but I don't want to be a man: Writing us-Chica-nos (Girl, Us)/Chicanas-into the movement script', in L. Grossberg, C. Nelson and P.A. Treichler (eds) *Cultural Studies*, London: Routledge.

Cherry, F. (1980) 'Ethnicity and language as indicants of social psychological status', in H. Giles (ed.) *Language: Social Psychological Perspectives*, Oxford: Pergamon.

——(1983) 'Gender roles and sexual violence', in E.R. Allgeier and N.B. McCormick (eds) *Changing Boundaries: Gender Roles and Sexual Behavior*, Palo Alto, Ca.: Mayfield Publishing.

——(1989) 'The textbook genre: an overview of its place in the knowledge industry', paper given at Canadian Psychological Association, Halifax, June.

Cherry, F. and Corkery, E. (1986) 'The role of textbooks in creating the history of a scientific social psychology', paper given at Canadian Psychological Association, Toronto, June.

Cherry, F. and Duncan, K. (1980) Children's sensitivity to gender-appropriate behaviour', paper given at Canadian Psychological Association, Calgary, June.

Clark, L. and Lewis, D. (1977) *Rape: The Price of Coercive Sexuality*, Toronto: The Women's Press.

Collier, G., Minton, H. L. and Reynolds, G. (1991) *Currents of Thought in American Social Psychology*, New York: Oxford University Press.

Constantinople, A. (1973) 'Masculinity–femininity: An exception to a famous dictum?', *Psychological Bulletin* 80: 389–407.

Corkery, E. (1986) 'The role of introductory textbooks in the portrayal of social psychology as a natural science', unpublished BA Honours thesis, Carleton University.

Cornwell, D., Hobbs, S. and Prytula, R. (1980) 'Little Albert rides again', *American Psychologist* 34: 216–17.

Cross, W.E., Jr (1978) 'Models of psychological nigrescence: a literature review', *Journal of Black Psychology* 5: 13–31.

——(1991) *Shades of Black: Diversity in African-American Identity*, Philadelphia: Temple University Press.

Danziger, K. (1984) 'Towards a conceptual framework for a critical history of psychology', in H. Carpintero and J.M. Peiro (eds) *Psychology in its Historical Context*, Valencia: Monografias de la Revista de Historia de la Psicologia.

——(1985) 'The origins of the psychological experiment as a social institution', *American Psychologist* 40: 133–40.

——(1990) *Constructing the Subject: Historical Origins of Psychological Research*, Cambridge: Cambridge University Press.

Davis, A. (1981) *Women, Race and Class*, New York: Random House.

Duchemin, P. (1988) 'Stealing history', *Briarpatch*, October: 17–23, Regina, Saskatchewan.

Duncan, K. (1980) 'Parental identification among preschoolers', unpublished BA Honours thesis, Carleton University.

Dutton, D. (1986) 'Wife assaulters' explanations for assault: The neutralization of self-punishment', *Canadian Journal of Behavioural Science* 18: 381–90.

Echols, A. (1989) *'Daring to be Bad': Radical Feminism in America, 1967–75*, Minneapolis: University of Minnesota Press.

Eisenhart, R.W. (1975) 'You can't hack it little girl: a discussion of the covert psychological agenda of modern combat training', *Journal of Social Issues* 31: 13–24.

Elms, A.C. (1972) *Social Psychology and Social Relevance*, Boston: Little Brown.

——(1975) 'The crisis of confidence in social psychology', *American Psychologist* 30: 967–76.

Evans, R. (1980) *The Making of Social Psychology*, New York: Gardner Press.

Feild, H.S. (1978) 'Attitudes toward rape: A comparative analysis of police, rapists, crisis counsellors, and citizens', *Journal of Personality and Social Psychology* 36: 1344–60.

Festinger, L. and Kelly, H.H. (1951) *Changing Attitudes through Social Contact: An Experimental Study of a Housing Project*, University of Michigan, Ann Arbor: Research Center for Group Dynamics, Institute for Social Research.

Festinger, L., Riecken, H.W. and Schachter, S. (1956) *When Prophecy Fails*, Minneapolis: University of Minnesota Press.

Festinger, L., Schachter, S. and Back, K. (1950) *Social Pressures in Informal Groups: A Study of Human Factors in Housing*, New York: Harper & Brothers.

Festinger, L., Cartwright, D., Barber, K., Fleischl, J., Gottsdanker, J., Keysen, A. and Leavitt, G. (1948) 'The study of rumour, its origins and spread', *Human Relations* 1: 464–86.

Findley, M. and Cooper, H. (1981) 'Introductory social psychology textbook citations: a comparison of five research areas', *Personality and Social Psychology Bulletin* 7: 173–6.

Finison, L. (1983) 'Origin myths and the teaching of social psychology', *Teaching of Psychology* 10: 29–30.

Friedan, B. (1963) *The Feminine Mystique*, New York: W.W. Norton.

Frodi, A., Macaulay, J. and Thome, P.R. (1977) 'Are women always less aggressive than men? A review of the experimental literature', *Psychological Bulletin* 84: 634–60.

Gergen, K. (1973) 'Social psychology as history', *Journal of Personality and Social Psychology* 26: 309–20.

——(1978) 'Toward generative theory', *Journal of Personality and Social Psychology* 36: 1344–60.

Gould, S.J. (1981) *The Mismeasure of Man*, New York: Norton & Co.

Graumann, C.F. (1988) 'Introduction to a history of social psychology', in M. Hewstone, W. Stroebe, J.-P. Codol and G.M. Stephenson (eds) *Introduction to Social Psychology: A European Perspective*, Oxford: Basil Blackwell.

Gregory, D. (1962) *From the Back of the Bus*, New York: Avon Books.

Griffin, C. (1989) 'I'm not a women's libber but . . .: feminism, consciousness and identity', in S. Skevington and D. Baker (eds) *The Social Identity of Women*, London: Sage.

Griffin, S. (1971) 'Rape: The all-American crime', *Ramparts*, September: 26–35.

Gross, A. (1978) 'The male role and heterosexual behaviour', in J.H. Pleck and R. Brannon (eds) *Male Roles and the Male Experience, Journal of Social Issues* 34: 87–107.

Haines, H. and Vaughan, G.M. (1979) 'Was 1898 a "great date" in the history of experimental social psychology?', *Journal of the History of the Behavioral Sciences* 15: 323–32.

Hall, W.S., Cross, W.E., Jr. and Freedle, R. (1972) 'Stages in the development of black awareness: an exploratory investigation', in R. Jones (ed.) *Black Psychology*, 1st edn, New York: Harper & Row.

Harari, H., Harari, O. and White, R.B. (1985) 'The reaction to rape by American male bystanders', The *Journal of Social Psychology* 125: 653–8.

Harding, S. (1987) 'Is there a feminist method?', in S. Harding (ed.) *Feminism and Methodology*, Bloomington, Ind.: Indiana University Press and Milton Keynes: Open University Press.

Harris, B. (1979) 'Whatever happened to Little Albert?', *American Psychologist* 34: 151–60.

——(1983) 'Telling students about the history of social psychology', *Teaching of Psychology* 10: 26–8.

Henriques, J., Hollway, W., Urwin, C., Venn, C. and Walkerdine, V. (1984) *Changing the Subject: Psychology, Social Regulation and Subjectivity*, London: Methuen.

Hilgard, E.R. (1987) *Psychology in America*, New York: Harcourt, Brace & Jovanovitch.

Hilgard, E.R., Leary, D. and McGuire, G. (1991) 'The history of psychology: a survey and critical assessment', *Annual Review of Psychology* 42: 79–107.

hooks, b. (1984) *Feminist Theory: From Margin to Center*, Boston: South End Press.

——(1990) *Yearning: Race, Gender and Cultural Politics*, Toronto: Between the Lines.

Israel, J. and Tajfel, H. (eds) (1972) *The Context of Social Psychology: A Critical Assessment*, London: Academic Press.

Jenni, D.A. and Jenni, M.A. (1976) 'Carrying behavior in humans: analysis of sex differences', *Science* 194: 859–60.

Jones, E.E. (1985a) 'Major developments in social psychology during the past five decades', in G. Lindzey and E. Aronson (eds) *Handbook of Social Psychology*, 3rd edn, New York: Random House.

——(1985b) 'History of social psychology', in G.A. Kimble and K. Schlesinger (eds) *Topics in the History of Psychology*, Hillsdale, N.J.: Lawrence Erlbaum.

Index

Index

Jones, R. (1985) *Research Methods in the Social and Behavioral Sciences*, Sunderland, Ma.: Sinauer Associates, Inc.

Jones, R.L. (1978) *Black Psychology*, 2nd edn, New York: Harper & Row.

Kanin, E. (1969) 'Selected dyadic aspects of male sex aggression', *Journal of Sex Research* 5: 12–28.

Kelly, B. (1950) 'Introduction', in L. Festinger, S. Schachter and K. Back (eds) *Social Pressures in Informal Groups*, New York: Harper & Brothers.

Kidder, L.H. and Fine, M. (1986) 'Making sense of injustice: social explanations, social action, and the role of the social scientist', in E. Seidman and J. Rappaport (eds) *Redefining Social Problems*, New York: Plenum Press.

Kirkpatrick, C. and Kanin, E. (1957) 'Male sex aggression on a university campus', *American Sociological Review* 22: 52–8.

Knorr-Cetina, K. (1981) *The Manufacture of Knowledge*, Oxford: Pergamon Press.

Kroch, A.S. (1979) 'Dialect and style in the speech of upper-class Philadelphia', paper given at International Conference on Social Psychology and Language, University of Bristol, July.

Lakeman, L. (1990) 'Women, violence and the Montreal massacre', *This Magazine* 23: 20–3, Toronto.

——(1990) 'Last words from a woman hater', *Globe and Mail*, 27 November 1990.

Latané, B. (1981) 'The psychology of social impact', *American Psychologist* 36: 343–56.

Latané, B. and Darley, J.M. (1970) *The Unresponsive Bystander: Why Doesn't He Help?*, New York: Meredith.

Latané, B. and Nida, S. (1981) 'Ten years of research on group size and helping', *Psychological Bulletin* 89: 308–24.

Latour, B. and Woolgar, S. (1979) *Laboratory Life: The Social Construction of Scientific Facts*, Beverly Hills, Ca.: Sage.

Levine, N. (1976) 'On the metaphysics of social psychology: A critical view', *Human Relations* 29: 385–400.

Lewis, H. (1972) *I Might as Well Move to the Moon: A Case Study on Housing Discrimination and a Legal Manual*, Bloomington, Ind.: Latino Affairs Publication of Indiana University.

Lott, B. (1985) 'The potential enrichment of social/personality psychology through feminist research and vice-versa', *American Psychologist* 40: 155–64.

Lottes, Ilsa L. (1988) 'Sexual socialization and attitudes towards rape', in A.W. Burgess (ed.) *Rape and Sexual Assault II*, New York: Garland Publishing, Inc.

Lubek, I. (1993a) 'Some reflections on various social psychologies, their histories and historiographies', *Sociétés Contemporaines* 13: 33–68.

——(1993b) 'Social psychology textbooks: An historical and social psychological analysis of conceptual filtering, consensus formation, career gatekeeping and conservatism in science', in H. Stam, L. Mos, W. Thorngate and B. Kaplan (eds) *Recent Trends in Theoretical Psychology*, vol. 3, New York: Springer-Verlag.

Lynn, D.B. and De Palma Cross, A. (1974) 'Parent preference of preschool children', *Journal of Marriage and the Family* 36: 555–9.

Macaulay, J. (1985) 'Adding gender to aggression research: incremental or revolutionary change?', in V.E. O'Leary, R.K. Unger and B.S. Wallston (eds) *Women, Gender and Social Psychology*, Hillsdale, NJ: Lawrence Erlbaum.

Maccoby, E.E. and Jacklin, C.N. (1974) *The Psychology of Sex Differences*, Stanford, Ca.: Stanford University Press.

Malamuth, N.M. (1981) 'Rape proclivity among males', *Journal of Social Issues* 37: 138–57.

McArthur, T. (1986) *Worlds of Reference: Lexicography, Learning and Language from the Clay Tablet to the Computer*, Cambridge: Cambridge University Press.

McGuire, W.J. (1983) 'A contextualist theory of knowledge: its implications for innovation and reform in psychological research', in L. Berkowitz (ed.) *Advances in Experimental Social Psychology*, New York: Academic Press.

McKeachie, W.J. (1976) 'Textbooks: Problems of publishers and professors', *Teaching of Psychology* 3: 29–30.

McNaught, K.W. and Cook, R. (1963) *Canada and the United States: A Modern Study*, Toronto: Clarke, Irwin & Co.

Mednick, M. (1989) 'On the politics of psychological constructs', *American Psychologist* 44: 1118–23.

Minton, H.L. (1984) 'J.F. Brown's social psychology of the 1930s: a historical antecedent to the contemporary crisis in social psychology', *Personality and Social Psychology Bulletin* 10: 31–42.

Moghaddam, F.M. (1987) 'Psychology in three worlds: as reflected by the crisis in social psychology and the move toward indigenous third-world psychology', *American Psychologist* 42: 912–20.

Morawski, J. (ed.) (1988) *The Rise of Experimentation in American Psychology*, New Haven, Conn.: Yale University Press.

Mussen, P.H. (1969) 'Early sex-role development', in D.A. Goslin (ed.) *Handbook of Socialization Theory and Research*, Chicago: Rand McNally.

Naylor, D. (1990) 'The delusions of one "artist"', *The Charlatan* (Carleton University) 25 October 1990: 12.

Nicholson, I. (1991) 'Harbinger of change: Goodwin Watson and the social engineering ideal', unpublished MA thesis, Carleton University.

Olson, D. (1980) 'On the language and authority of textbooks', *Journal of Communication* 30: 186–96.

Parker, I. (1989) *The Crisis in Modern Social Psychology, and How to End It*, London: Routledge.

Parlee, M.B. (1979) 'Psychology and women', *Signs* 5: 121–33.

Patnoe, S. (1988) *A Narrative History of Experimental Social Psychology: The Lewin Tradition*, New York: Springer-Verlag.

Paul, D. (1987) 'The nine lives of discredited data: old textbooks never die – they just get paraphrased', *The Sciences* 27: 26–30.

Potter, J. and Wetherell, M. (1987) *Discourse and Social Psychology*, London: Sage.

Quereshi, N.Y. and Sackett, P.R. (1977) 'An updated content analysis of introductory psychology textbooks', *Teaching of Psychology* 4: 25–30.

Quereshi, N.Y. and Zulli, M.R. (1975) 'A content analysis of introductory psychology textbooks', *Teaching of Psychology* 2: 60–65.

Rebecca, M., Hefner, R. and Oleshansky, B. (1976) 'A model of sex-role transcendence', *Journal of Social Issues* 32: 197–206.

Rendon, A.R. (1971) *Chicano Manifesto*, New York: Macmillan.

Rogers, A. and Bowie, J.A. (1984) 'Directory of introductory psychology textbooks in print', *Teaching of Psychology* 11: 59–62.

Rohrer, J.H. and Sherif, M. (1953) *Groups in Harmony and Tension: An Integration of Studies in Intergroup Relations*, New York: Harper & Bros.

Rosenthal, A. M. (1964) *Thirty-Eight Witnesses*, New York: McGraw-Hill.

Rothman, R.A. (1971) 'Textbooks and the certification of knowledge', *The American Sociologist* 6: 126–7.

Rudmin, F. (1985) 'William McDougall in the history of social psychology', *British Journal of Social Psychology* 24: 75–6.

Samelson, F. (1974) 'History, origin myth and ideology: Comte's "discovery" of social psychology', *Journal for the Theory of Social Behaviour* 4: 217–31.

——(1980) 'J. B. Watson's Little Albert, Cyril Burt's twins, and the need for critical science', *American Psychologist* 35: 619–25.

——(1986) 'Authoritarianism from Berlin to Berkeley: on social psychology and history', *Journal of Social Issues* 42: 191–208.

Sampson, E. (1971) *Social Psychology and Contemporary Society*, New York: Wiley.

——(1977) 'Psychology and the American ideal', *Journal of Personality and Social Psychology* 35: 767–82.

Samuel, W. (1975) *Contemporary Social Psychology: An Introduction*, Englewood Cliffs, NJ: Prentice-Hall.

Schau, C., Kahn, L., Diepold, J.H. and Cherry, F. (1980) 'The relationship of parental expectations and preschool children's verbal sex-typing to their sex-typed play behavior', *Child Development* 51: 266–70.

Schechter, S. (1982) *Women and Male Violence*, Boston: South End Press.

Schreiber, E. (1979) 'Bystander's intervention in situations of violence', *Psychological Reports* 45: 243–6.

Secord, P.F. and Backman, C.W. (1964) *Social Psychology*, New York: McGraw-Hill.

Segal, L. (1987) *Is the Future Female? Troubled Thoughts on Contemporary Feminism*, London: Virago Press.

Shaver, K.G. (1977) *Principles of Social Psychology*, Cambridge, Ma.: Winthrop.

Sheilds, S.A. (1975) 'Functionalism, Darwinism, and the psychology of women: a study in social myth', *American Psychologist* 30: 739–54.

Sherif, C.W. (1976) *Orientation in Social Psychology*, New York: Harper & Row.

——(1979) 'Bias in psychology', in J. Sherman and E.T. Beck (eds) *The Prism of Sex: Essays in the Sociology of Knowledge*, Madison: University of Wisconsin Press.

Sherif, M. (1954) 'Integrating field work and laboratory work in small group research', *American Sociological Review* 19: 759–71.

——(1956) 'Experiments in group conflict', *Scientific American* 195 (5).

——(1958) 'Superordinate goals in the reduction of conflict', *American Journal of Sociology* 63: 349–56.

——(1967) *Social Interaction: Process and Products*, Chicago: Aldine Publishing.

Sherif, M. and Sherif, C.W. (1953) *Groups in Harmony and Tension: An Integration of Studies in Intergroup Relations*, New York: Harper & Bros.

——(1956) *An Outline of Social Psychology*, 2nd edn, New York: Harper & Bros.

——(1969) *An Outline of Social Psychology*, 3rd edn, New York: Harper & Row.

Sherif, M., White, B.J. and Harvey, D.J. (1955) 'Status relations in experimentally produced groups through judgmental indices', *American Journal of Sociology* 50, 370–9.

Sherif, M., Harvey, D.J., White, B.J., Hood, W.R. and Sherif, C.W. (1954) 'Study of positive and negative intergroup attitudes between experimentally produced groups', *Robbers' Cave Study*, Norman, Oklahoma: University of Oklahoma.

Sherif, M., Harvey, D.J., White, B.J., Hood, W.R. and Sherif, C.W. (1961) *Intergroup Conflict and Cooperation: The Robbers' Cave Experiment*, publication of the Institute of Group Relations, Norman, Oklahoma.

Shotland, R.L. and Straw, M.K. (1976) 'Bystander response to an assault: when a man attacks a woman', *Journal of Personality and Social Psychology* 34: 990–9.

Smith, V. (1990) 'Split affinities: the case of interracial rape', in M. Hirsch and E.F. Keller (eds) *Conflicts in Feminism*, New York: Routledge.

Strickland, L. (1991) 'Russian and Soviet psychology', *Canadian Psychology* 32: 580–93.

Strickland, L., Aboud, F. and Gergen, K. (1976) *Social Psychology in Transition*, New York: Plenum Publishing.

Stringer, P. (1990) 'Prefacing social psychology: a textbook example', in I. Parker and J. Shotter (eds) *Deconstructing Social Psychology*, London: Routledge.

Tivers, J. (1985) *Women Attached: The Daily Lives of Women with Young Children*, London: Croom Helm.

Unterecker, J. (1973) 'Foreword', in E. Schlossberg, *Einstein and Beckett: A Record of an Imaginary Discussion with Albert Einstein and Samuel Beckett*, New York: Links Books.

Venn, C. (1984) 'The subject of psychology', in J. Henriques, W. Hollway, C. Urwin, C. Venn and V. Walkerdine (eds) *Changing the Subject: Psychology, Social Regulation and Subjectivity*, London: Methuen.

Walker, L. (1984) *The Battered Woman Syndrome*, New York: Springer.

Wallston, B.S. and Grady, K.E. (1985) 'Integrating the feminist critique and the crisis in social psychology: another look at research methods', in V.E. O'Leary, R.K. Unger and B.S. Wallston (eds) *Women, Gender and Social Psychology*, Hillsdale, NJ: Lawrence Erlbaum.

Watson, J.B. and Rayner, R. (1920) 'Conditioned emotional reactions', *Journal of Experimental Psychology* 3: 1–14.

Weatherford, J. (1988) *Indian Givers: How the Indians of the Americas Transformed the World*, New York: Fawcett Columbine.

Weisstein, N. (1970) 'Psychology constructs the female, or the fantasy life of the male psychologist', in M.H. Garskof (ed.) *Roles Women Play: Readings toward Women's Liberation*, Belmont, Ca.: Brooks Cole.

Wilkinson, N. and Schneider, M. (1990) 'The development of a feminist consciousness in women', paper given at Canadian Psychological Association, Ottawa, June.

Wilkinson, S. (1986) *Feminist Social Psychology*, Philadelphia, Pa.: Open University Press.

Wittman, C. (1972) 'Refugees from Amerika: a gay manifesto', in C. Wittman (ed.) *The Homosexual Dialectic*, Englewood Cliffs, NJ: Prentice-Hall. First published in the San Francisco Free Press (22 December–7 January 1969–70).

Wright, R. (1992) *Stolen Continents: The 'New World' Through Indian Eyes*, Toronto: Penguin Books.

Wrightsman, L. and Deaux, K. (1981) *Social Psychology in the 1980s*, 3rd edn, Monterey, Ca.: Brooks Cole Publishing Co.

Wyburn, B.M., Pickford, R.W. and Hirst, R.J. (1964) *Human Senses and Perception*, Toronto: University of Toronto Press.

Ziman, J.M. (1976) *The Force of Knowledge: The Scientific Dimension of Society*, Cambridge: Cambridge University Press.